The Thinking Tree
Summer & Winter
OLYMPIC SPORTS
Research Handbook

Study 60 Different Sports

Social Studies, History, Geography & Math!

The Thinking Tree
SUMMER & WINTER
OLYMPIC SPORTS

Study 60 Different Sports

This Book Belongs to:

By: Sarah Janisse Brown
Artwork by Rachel Brown
Designed by Susannah Brown
Math & Research Prompts By: Jody LeDuc Smith & Janet Salut

FunSchooling.com

Copyright 2022 - Copies allowed for Household Use
The Thinking Tree, LLC — Dyslexie Font

Table of Contents:

About This Book 5
Olympic History 6
Winter & Summer Sports 8
Winning Countries 10
Olympic World Map 16
Acrobatic Gymnastics 20
Alpine Skiing 24
Archery 28
Artistic Gymnastics 32
Artistic Swimming 36
Athletics 40
Badminton 44
Baseball/Softball 48
Basketball 52
Beach Handball 56
Beach Volleyball 60
Biathlon 64
BMX Freestyle 68
BMX Racing 72
Bobsleigh 76
Boxing 80
Breaking 84
Canoe Kayak Flatwater 88
Canoe Kayak Slalom 92
Curling 96
Diving 100
Fencing 104
Figure Skating 108
Football 114
Freestyle Skiing 118
Futsal 122
Golf 126
Handball 130
Hockey 134
Karate 138

Luge 142
Marathon Swimming 146
Modern Pentathlon 150
Mountain Bike 154
Nordic Combined 158
Rhythmic Gymnastics 162
Roller Speed Skating 166
Rowing 170
Rugby 174
Shooting 178
Short Track Speed Skating 182
Skateboarding 186
Skeleton 190
Ski Jumping 194
Ski Mountaineering 198
Snow Boarding 202
Speed Skating 206
Sport Climbing 210
Surfing 214
Table Tennis 218
Tae Kwon Do 222
Tennis 226
Track 230
Track Cycling 234
Trampoline 238
Triathlon 242
Volleyball 246
Water Polo 250
Weightlifting 254
Wrestling 258
Extra Sports 262
Math Mysteries 275
Favorite Olympic Sports 292
Research Challenge Key 295

About this Book:

Welcome to the Olympics!

This book will help you discover many of the sports and events which are included in both the Summer and Winter Olympic Games. As you work through the pages you can research past Olympics or the current games!

Choose some library books, check approved internet sources, find some past videos, or even watch some awesome movies to learn more about the Olympics.

Study the origin of the Olympic Games, research the players, learn more about the events in which they participate!

You will be learning about Sports, History, Social Studies, Research Skills, Geography, and Math.

Materials Needed:

Colored Pencils
Pencils
Gel Pens
Access to the internet for research.
Books & documentaries about Olympic sports.
A viewing device (TV, Computer or Tablet)

Research Olympic History And Share Three Interesting Facts:

1. _____
_____
_____
_____
_____

2. _____
_____
_____
_____
_____
_____

3. _____
_____
_____
_____
_____
_____

Why do we call this event "The Olympics?"

_____
_____
_____

What can you learn about the first Olympic Games in 776 BCE?

_____
_____
_____
_____

Illustrate the First Olympic Games

What Sports are Featured during the Winter Olympics?

What Sports are Featured during the Summer Olympics?

List the Countries who won the most Medals
Winter Olympics

YEAR:____ Location:_____

Name of Country	Gold	Silver	Bronze

LIST THE COUNTRIES WHO WON THE MOST MEDALS
SUMMER OLYMPICS

YEAR:____ Location:_____

Name of Country	Gold	Silver	Bronze

List the Countries who won the most Medals
Winter Olympics

YEAR:_____ Location:_____

Name of Country	Gold	Silver	Bronze

List the Countries who won the most Medals
SUMMER OLYMPICS

YEAR: _____ Location: _____

Name of Country	Gold	Silver	Bronze

List the Countries who won the most Medals
Winter Olympics

YEAR:____ Location:_____

Name of Country	Gold	Silver	Bronze

List the Countries who won the most Medals

SUMMER OLYMPICS

YEAR:____ Location:_____

Name of Country	Gold	Silver	Bronze

Draw a DOT on each city that has hosted
THE OLYMPIC GAMES

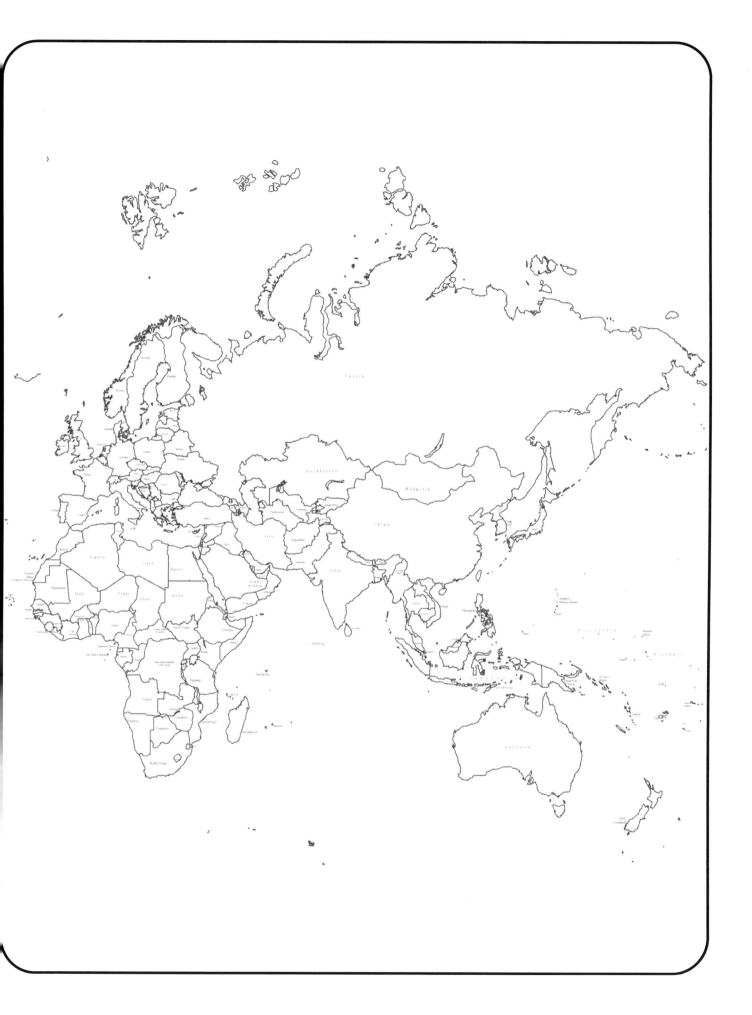

The Thinking Tree
OLYMPICS SPORTS
Research Guide

Study 60 Different Sports
From the Winter & Summer Games

Acrobatic Gymnastics

Who were the winners in the most recent Olympics?

Medal	Men's Competition	Score	Women's Competition	Score
Gold				
Silver				
Bronze				

Research Challenge

Acrobatic Gymnastics
What is the code of points
and how has it changed over the years?

Design Challenge

Design a competition area, playing field, equipment,
or score board for this sport:

Sport Study
Acrobatic Gymnastics

It's research time!
Use the Internet, books, tutorials and documentaries to study this sport. Or go see a game or competition!

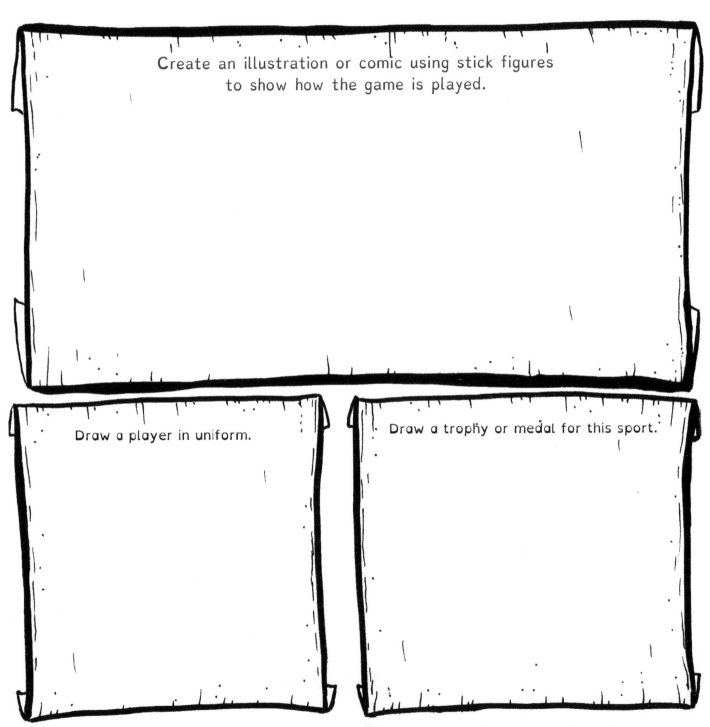

Create an illustration or comic using stick figures to show how the game is played.

Draw a player in uniform.

Draw a trophy or medal for this sport.

If you don't enjoy drawing, you may print, cut, and paste photos from the internet or a magazine onto this page.

Where did this sport originate?
_____
_____

How was this sport invented?
_____
_____
_____
_____

Who are the main sponsors of the events for this sport?
_____
_____

What is the name of the largest competition where this sport is played? _____
_____
_____
_____
_____
_____

Who is the #1 player of this sport? What makes them the best? How much money do they earn? Where do their earnings come from?
_____
_____
_____
_____

Would you like to play this sport? Why or why not?
_____
_____

What are the common injuries from playing this sport?
_____
_____
_____

What is a random fact about this sport?
_____
_____
_____

Alpine Skiing

Who were the winners in the most recent Olympics?

Medal	Men's Competition	Score	Women's Competition	Score
Gold				
Silver				
Bronze				

Research Challenge

Alpine Skiing
What is the primary difference between
Alpine Skiing and other types of skiing?

Design Challenge

Design a competition area, playing field, equipment,
or score board for this sport:

Sport Study
Alpine Skiing

It's research time!
Use the Internet, books, tutorials and documentaries to study this sport. Or go see a game or competition!

Create an illustration or comic using stick figures to show how the game is played.

Draw a player in uniform.

Draw a trophy or medal for this sport.

If you don't enjoy drawing, you may print, cut, and paste photos from the internet or a magazine onto this page.

Where did this sport originate?
_____
_____

How was this sport invented?
_____
_____
_____

Who are the main sponsors of the events for this sport?
_____
_____

What is the name of the largest competition where this sport is played? _____
_____
_____
_____
_____

Who is the #1 player of this sport? What makes them the best? How much money do they earn? Where do their earnings come from?
_____
_____
_____
_____

Would you like to play this sport? Why or why not?
_____
_____

What are the common injuries from playing this sport?
_____
_____
_____

What is a random fact about this sport?
_____
_____
_____

Archery

Who were the winners in the most recent Olympics?

Medal	Men's Competition	Score	Women's Competition	Score
Gold				
Silver				
Bronze				

Research Challenge

How many circles are on an Olympic target and how large in diameter is the target face?

Design Challenge

Design a competition area, playing field, equipment, or score board for this sport:

Sport Study
Archery

It's research time!
Use the Internet, books, tutorials and documentaries to study this sport. Or go see a game or competition!

Create an illustration or comic using stick figures to show how the game is played.

Draw a player in uniform.

Draw a trophy or medal for this sport.

If you don't enjoy drawing, you may print, cut, and paste photos from the internet or a magazine onto this page.

Where did this sport originate?
_____
_____

How was this sport invented?
_____
_____
_____
_____

Who are the main sponsors of the events for this sport?
_____
_____
_____

What is the name of the largest competition where this sport is played? _____
_____
_____
_____
_____

Who is the #1 player of this sport? What makes them the best? How much money do they earn? Where do their earnings come from?
_____
_____
_____
_____
_____

Would you like to play this sport? Why or why not?
_____
_____
_____

What are the common injuries from playing this sport?
_____
_____
_____
_____

What is a random fact about this sport?
_____
_____
_____
_____

Artistic Gymnastics

Who were the winners in the most recent Olympics?

Medal	Men's Competition	Score	Women's Competition	Score
Gold				
Silver				
Bronze				

Research Challenge

Artistic Gymnastics

What three things are both male and female gymnasts judged on?

_____
_____
_____
_____
_____
_____

Design Challenge

Design a competition area, playing field, equipment, or score board for this sport:

Sport Study
Artistic Gymnastics

It's research time!
Use the Internet, books, tutorials and documentaries to study this sport. Or go see a game or competition!

Create an illustration or comic using stick figures to show how the game is played.

Draw a player in uniform.

Draw a trophy or medal for this sport.

If you don't enjoy drawing, you may print, cut, and paste photos from the internet or a magazine onto this page.

Where did this sport originate?
_____
_____

How was this sport invented?
_____
_____
_____

Who are the main sponsors of the events for this sport?
_____
_____

What is the name of the largest competition where this sport is played? _____
_____
_____
_____
_____

Who is the #1 player of this sport? What makes them the best? How much money do they earn? Where do their earnings come from?
_____
_____
_____
_____

Would you like to play this sport? Why or why not?
_____
_____

What are the common injuries from playing this sport?
_____
_____
_____

What is a random fact about this sport?
_____
_____
_____

Artistic Swimming

Who were the winners in the most recent Olympics?

Medal	Men's Competition	Score	Women's Competition	Score
Gold				
Silver				
Bronze				

Research Challenge

Artistic Swimming
What is another name for Artistic Swimming?
What other name was it known by?

Design Challenge

Design a competition area, playing field, equipment, or score board for this sport:

Sport Study
Artistic Swimming

It's research time!
Use the Internet, books, tutorials and documentaries to study this sport. Or go see a game or competition!

Create an illustration or comic using stick figures to show how the game is played.

Draw a player in uniform.

Draw a trophy or medal for this sport.

If you don't enjoy drawing, you may print, cut, and paste photos from the internet or a magazine onto this page.

Where did this sport originate?
_____
_____

How was this sport invented?
_____
_____
_____

Who are the main sponsors of the events for this sport?
_____
_____

What is the name of the largest competition where this sport is played? _____
_____
_____
_____
_____

Who is the #1 player of this sport? What makes them the best? How much money do they earn? Where do their earnings come from?
_____
_____
_____
_____

Would you like to play this sport? Why or why not?
_____
_____

What are the common injuries from playing this sport?
_____
_____
_____

What is a random fact about this sport?
_____
_____
_____

Athletics

Note: Athletics refers to the field events at a track meet! Focus your research on the strength and throwing events in this section. There will be a section for the races later on in this book.

Who were the winners in the most recent Olympics?

Medal	Men's Competition	Score	Women's Competition	Score
Gold				
Silver				
Bronze				

Research Challenge

Athletics
What three types of events are included in Athletics?

Design Challenge

Design a competition area, playing field, equipment, or score board for this sport:

Sport Study
Athletics

It's research time!
Use the Internet, books, tutorials and documentaries to study this sport. Or go see a game or competition!

Create an illustration or comic using stick figures to show how the game is played.

Draw a player in uniform.

Draw a trophy or medal for this sport.

If you don't enjoy drawing, you may print, cut, and paste photos from the internet or a magazine onto this page.

Where did this sport originate?
_____
_____

How was this sport invented?
_____
_____
_____

Who are the main sponsors of the events for this sport?
_____
_____

What is the name of the largest competition where this sport is played? _____
_____
_____
_____
_____

Who is the #1 player of this sport? What makes them the best? How much money do they earn? Where do their earnings come from?
_____
_____
_____
_____

Would you like to play this sport? Why or why not?
_____
_____

What are the common injuries from playing this sport?
_____
_____
_____

What is a random fact about this sport?
_____
_____
_____

Badminton

Who were the winners in the most recent Olympics?

Medal	Men's Competition	Score	Women's Competition	Score
Gold				
Silver				
Bronze				

Research Challenge

Badminton
What kind of scoring is used for Badminton?
What does this mean?

Design Challenge

Design a competition area, playing field, equipment, or score board for this sport:

Sport Study
Badminton

It's research time!
Use the Internet, books, tutorials and documentaries to study this sport. Or go see a game or competition!

Create an illustration or comic using stick figures to show how the game is played.

Draw a player in uniform.

Draw a trophy or medal for this sport.

If you don't enjoy drawing, you may print, cut, and paste photos from the internet or a magazine onto this page.

Where did this sport originate?
_____
_____

How was this sport invented?
_____
_____
_____

Who are the main sponsors of the events for this sport?
_____
_____

What is the name of the largest competition where this sport is played? _____
_____
_____
_____
_____

Who is the #1 player of this sport? What makes them the best? How much money do they earn? Where do their earnings come from?
_____
_____
_____
_____

Would you like to play this sport? Why or why not?
_____
_____

What are the common injuries from playing this sport?
_____
_____
_____

What is a random fact about this sport?
_____
_____
_____

Baseball & Softball

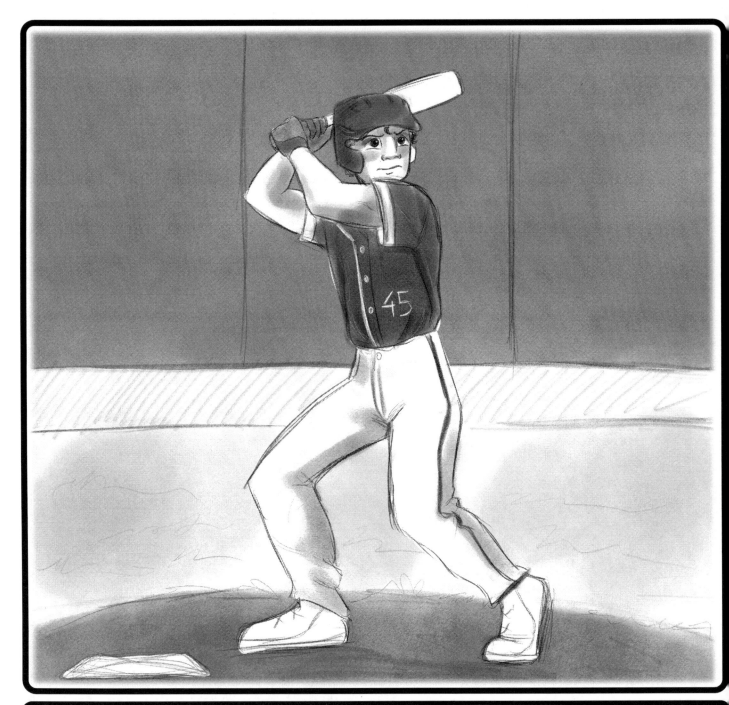

Who were the winners in the most recent Olympics?

Medal	Men's Competition	Score	Women's Competition	Score
Gold				
Silver				
Bronze				

Research Challenge

How are the qualifying teams decided
for the Olympic games? Do you think this is fair?

_____
_____
_____
_____
_____
_____
_____

Design Challenge

Design a competition area, playing field, equipment,
or score board for this sport:

Sport Study
Baseball & Softball

It's research time!
Use the Internet, books, tutorials and documentaries to study this sport. Or go see a game or competition!

Create an illustration or comic using stick figures to show how the game is played.

Draw a player in uniform.

Draw a trophy or medal for this sport.

If you don't enjoy drawing, you may print, cut, and paste photos from the internet or a magazine onto this page.

Where did this sport originate?
_____
_____

How was this sport invented?
_____
_____
_____

Who are the main sponsors of the events for this sport?
_____
_____

What is the name of the largest competition where this sport is played? _____
_____
_____
_____
_____

Who is the #1 player of this sport? What makes them the best? How much money do they earn? Where do their earnings come from?
_____
_____
_____
_____

Would you like to play this sport? Why or why not?
_____
_____

What are the common injuries from playing this sport?
_____
_____
_____

What is a random fact about this sport?
_____
_____
_____

Basketball

Who were the winners in the most recent Olympics?

Medal	Men's Competition	Score	Women's Competition	Score
Gold				
Silver				
Bronze				

Research Challenge

Basketball

What is a technical foul? How do you get one? What happens when the referee calls one against your team?

Design Challenge

Design a competition area, playing field, equipment, or score board for this sport:

Sport Study
Basketball

It's research time!
Use the Internet, books, tutorials and documentaries to study this sport. Or go see a game or competition!

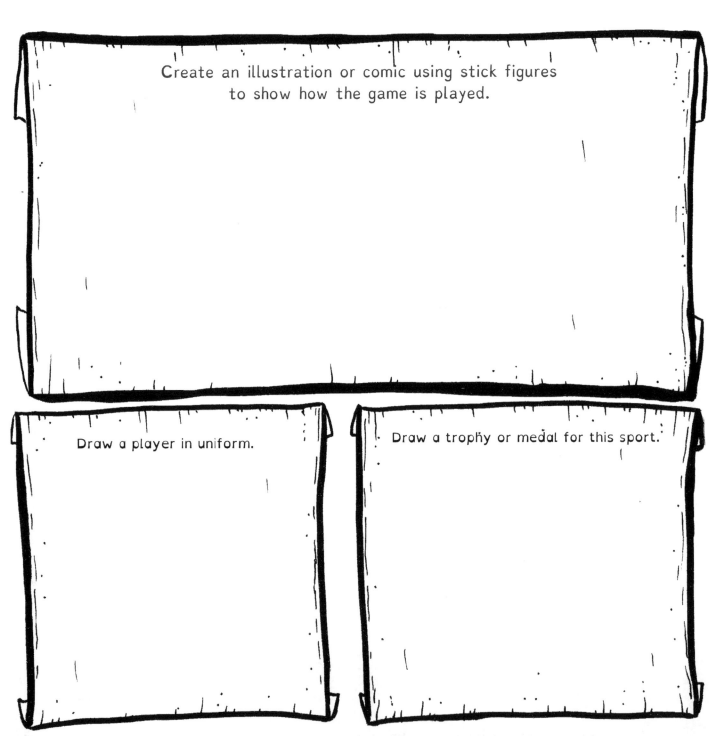

Create an illustration or comic using stick figures to show how the game is played.

Draw a player in uniform.

Draw a trophy or medal for this sport.

If you don't enjoy drawing, you may print, cut, and paste photos from the internet or a magazine onto this page.

Where did this sport originate?
_____
_____

How was this sport invented?
_____
_____
_____

Who are the main sponsors of the events for this sport?
_____
_____

What is the name of the largest competition where this sport is played? _____
_____
_____
_____
_____

Who is the #1 player of this sport? What makes them the best? How much money do they earn? Where do their earnings come from?
_____
_____
_____
_____

Would you like to play this sport? Why or why not?
_____
_____

What are the common injuries from playing this sport?
_____
_____
_____

What is a random fact about this sport?
_____
_____
_____

Beach Handball

Who were the winners in the most recent Olympics?

Medal	Men's Competition	Score	Women's Competition	Score
Gold				
Silver				
Bronze				

Research Challenge

Beach Handball
How does Beach Handball differ from standard Handball?
Do you think this makes it easier or more difficult?

_____
_____
_____
_____
_____
_____
_____

Design Challenge

Design a competition area, playing field, equipment, or score board for this sport:

Sport Study
Beach Handball

It's research time!
Use the Internet, books, tutorials and documentaries to study this sport. Or go see a game or competition!

Create an illustration or comic using stick figures to show how the game is played.

Draw a player in uniform.

Draw a trophy or medal for this sport.

If you don't enjoy drawing, you may print, cut, and paste photos from the internet or a magazine onto this page.

Where did this sport originate?
_____
_____

How was this sport invented?
_____
_____
_____

Who are the main sponsors of the events for this sport?
_____
_____

What is the name of the largest competition where this sport is played? _____
_____
_____
_____
_____

Who is the #1 player of this sport? What makes them the best? How much money do they earn? Where do their earnings come from?
_____
_____
_____
_____

Would you like to play this sport? Why or why not?
_____
_____

What are the common injuries from playing this sport?
_____
_____
_____

What is a random fact about this sport?
_____
_____
_____

Beach Volleyball

Who were the winners in the most recent Olympics?

Medal	Men's Competition	Score	Women's Competition	Score
Gold				
Silver				
Bronze				

Research Challenge

Beach Volleyball
How many teams take part in the Beach Volleyball tournament and is there a limit of teams for each country?

_____
_____
_____
_____
_____
_____

Design Challenge

Design a competition area, playing field, equipment, or score board for this sport:

Sport Study
Beach Volleyball

It's research time!
Use the Internet, books, tutorials and documentaries to study this sport. Or go see a game or competition!

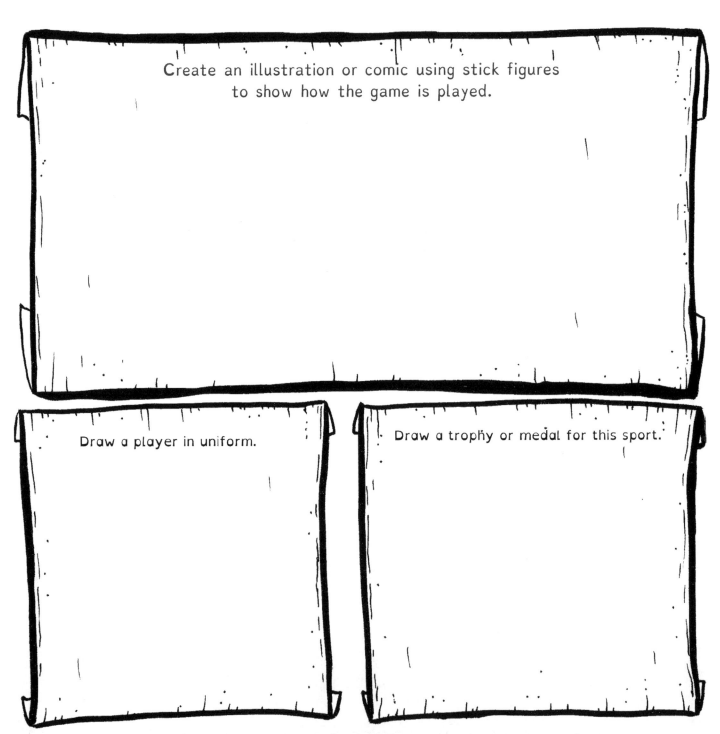

Create an illustration or comic using stick figures to show how the game is played.

Draw a player in uniform.

Draw a trophy or medal for this sport.

If you don't enjoy drawing, you may print, cut, and paste photos from the internet or a magazine onto this page.

Where did this sport originate?
_____
_____

How was this sport invented?
_____
_____
_____

Who are the main sponsors of the events for this sport?
_____
_____

What is the name of the largest competition where this sport is played? _____
_____
_____
_____
_____

Who is the #1 player of this sport? What makes them the best? How much money do they earn? Where do their earnings come from?
_____
_____
_____
_____

Would you like to play this sport? Why or why not?
_____
_____

What are the common injuries from playing this sport?
_____
_____
_____

What is a random fact about this sport?
_____
_____
_____

Biathlon

Who were the winners in the most recent Olympics?

Medal	Men's Competition	Score	Women's Competition	Score
Gold				
Silver				
Bronze				

Research Challenge

Biathalon

What two sports are combined to create the Biathlon competition?

Design Challenge

Design a competition area, playing field, equipment, or score board for this sport:

Sport Study
Biathlon

It's research time!
Use the Internet, books, tutorials and documentaries to study this sport. Or go see a game or competition!

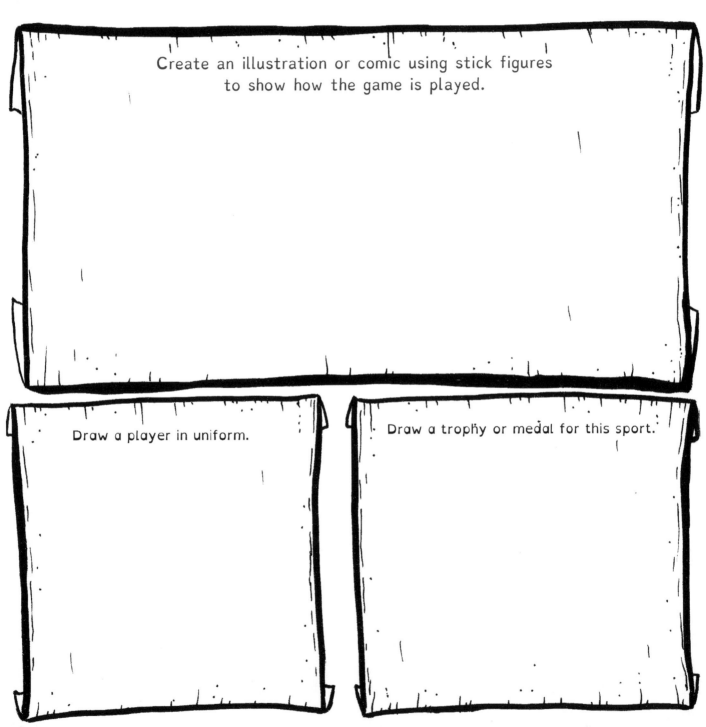

Create an illustration or comic using stick figures to show how the game is played.

Draw a player in uniform.

Draw a trophy or medal for this sport.

If you don't enjoy drawing, you may print, cut, and paste photos from the internet or a magazine onto this page.

Where did this sport originate?
_____
_____

How was this sport invented?
_____
_____
_____
_____

Who are the main sponsors of the events for this sport?
_____
_____
_____

What is the name of the largest competition where this sport is played? _____
_____
_____
_____
_____
_____

Who is the #1 player of this sport? What makes them the best? How much money do they earn? Where do their earnings come from?
_____
_____
_____
_____

Would you like to play this sport? Why or why not?
_____
_____

What are the common injuries from playing this sport?
_____
_____
_____

What is a random fact about this sport?
_____
_____
_____

BMX Freestyle

Who were the winners in the most recent Olympics?

Medal	Men's Competition	Score	Women's Competition	Score
Gold				
Silver				
Bronze				

Research Challenge

BMX Freestyle

Can you list 5 air tricks and 5 flatland tricks that an Olympian might use in the BMX freestyle competition?

_____
_____
_____
_____
_____
_____
_____
_____

Design Challenge

Design a competition area, playing field, equipment, or score board for this sport:

Sport Study
BMX Freestyle

It's research time!
Use the Internet, books, tutorials and documentaries to study this sport. Or go see a game or competition!

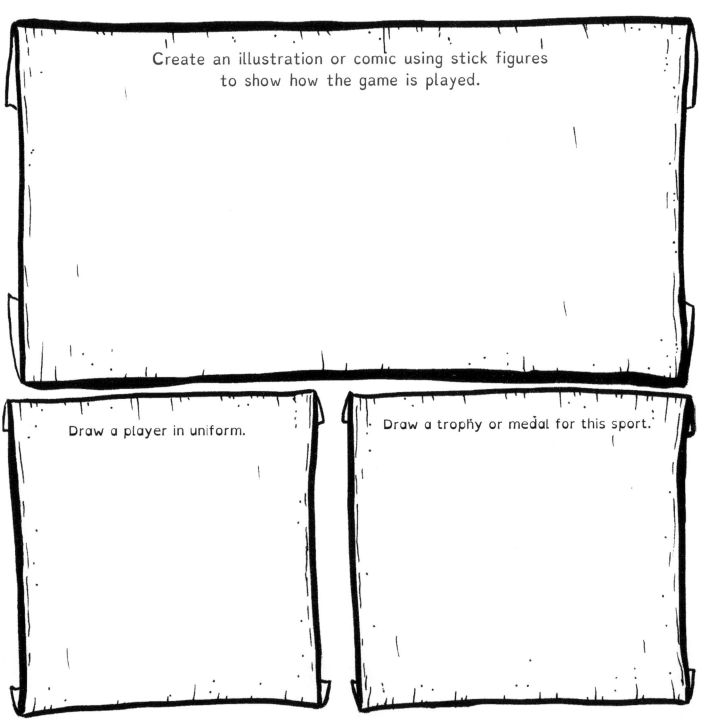

Create an illustration or comic using stick figures to show how the game is played.

Draw a player in uniform.

Draw a trophy or medal for this sport.

If you don't enjoy drawing, you may print, cut, and paste photos from the internet or a magazine onto this page.

Where did this sport originate?
_____
_____

How was this sport invented?
_____
_____
_____

Who are the main sponsors of the events for this sport?
_____
_____

What is the name of the largest competition where this sport is played? _____
_____
_____
_____
_____

Who is the #1 player of this sport? What makes them the best? How much money do they earn? Where do their earnings come from?
_____
_____
_____
_____

Would you like to play this sport? Why or why not?
_____
_____

What are the common injuries from playing this sport?
_____
_____
_____

What is a random fact about this sport?
_____
_____
_____

BMX Racing

Who were the winners in the most recent Olympics?

Medal	Men's Competition	Score	Women's Competition	Score
Gold				
Silver				
Bronze				

Research Challenge

BMX Racing
What are the three different rounds in the BMX Racing competition and how many cyclists compete in each?

Design Challenge

Design a competition area, playing field, equipment, or score board for this sport:

Sport Study
BMX Racing

It's research time!
Use the Internet, books, tutorials and documentaries to study this sport. Or go see a game or competition!

Create an illustration or comic using stick figures to show how the game is played.

Draw a player in uniform.

Draw a trophy or medal for this sport.

If you don't enjoy drawing, you may print, cut, and paste photos from the internet or a magazine onto this page.

Where did this sport originate?
_____
_____

How was this sport invented?
_____
_____
_____

Who are the main sponsors of the events for this sport?
_____
_____

What is the name of the largest competition where this sport is played? _____
_____
_____
_____
_____
_____

Who is the #1 player of this sport? What makes them the best? How much money do they earn? Where do their earnings come from?
_____
_____
_____
_____

Would you like to play this sport? Why or why not?
_____
_____

What are the common injuries from playing this sport?
_____
_____
_____

What is a random fact about this sport?
_____
_____
_____

Bobsleigh

Who were the winners in the most recent Olympics?

Medal	Men's Competition	Score	Women's Competition	Score
Gold				
Silver				
Bronze				

Research Challenge

Bobsleigh

Since being introduced at the 1912 games, what is the only year that this event has not been featured and why?

_____
_____
_____
_____
_____
_____
_____

Design Challenge

Design a competition area, playing field, equipment, or score board for this sport:

Sport Study
Bobsleigh

It's research time!
Use the Internet, books, tutorials and documentaries to study this sport. Or go see a game or competition!

Create an illustration or comic using stick figures to show how the game is played.

Draw a player in uniform.

Draw a trophy or medal for this sport.

If you don't enjoy drawing, you may print, cut, and paste photos from the internet or a magazine onto this page.

Where did this sport originate?
_____
_____

How was this sport invented?
_____
_____
_____

Who are the main sponsors of the events for this sport?
_____
_____

What is the name of the largest competition where this sport is played? _____
_____
_____
_____
_____

Who is the #1 player of this sport? What makes them the best? How much money do they earn? Where do their earnings come from?
_____
_____
_____
_____

Would you like to play this sport? Why or why not?
_____
_____

What are the common injuries from playing this sport?
_____
_____
_____

What is a random fact about this sport?
_____
_____
_____

Boxing

Who were the winners in the most recent Olympics?

Medal	Men's Competition	Score	Women's Competition	Score
Gold				
Silver				
Bronze				

Research Challenge

Boxing

What year did the Olympics incorporate women's Boxing as an Olympic event in addition to men's and how many weight classes does each consist of?

_____
_____
_____
_____
_____
_____
_____

Design Challenge

Design a competition area, playing field, equipment, or score board for this sport:

Sport Study
Boxing

It's research time!
Use the Internet, books, tutorials and documentaries to study this sport. Or go see a game or competition!

Create an illustration or comic using stick figures to show how the game is played.

Draw a player in uniform.

Draw a trophy or medal for this sport.

If you don't enjoy drawing, you may print, cut, and paste photos from the internet or a magazine onto this page.

Where did this sport originate?
_____
_____

How was this sport invented?
_____
_____
_____

Who are the main sponsors of the events for this sport?
_____
_____

What is the name of the largest competition where this sport is played? _____
_____
_____
_____
_____

Who is the #1 player of this sport? What makes them the best? How much money do they earn? Where do their earnings come from?
_____
_____
_____
_____

Would you like to play this sport? Why or why not?
_____
_____

What are the common injuries from playing this sport?
_____
_____
_____

What is a random fact about this sport?
_____
_____
_____

Breaking

Who were the winners in the most recent Olympics?

Medal	Men's Competition	Score	Women's Competition	Score
Gold				
Silver				
Bronze				

Research Challenge

Breaking

What was the first year that Olympics introduced Breaking (or breakdancing) to the summer Olympic program and how many were competing?

Design Challenge

Design a competition area, playing field, equipment, or score board for this sport:

Sport Study
Breaking

It's research time!
Use the Internet, books, tutorials and documentaries to study this sport. Or go see a game or competition!

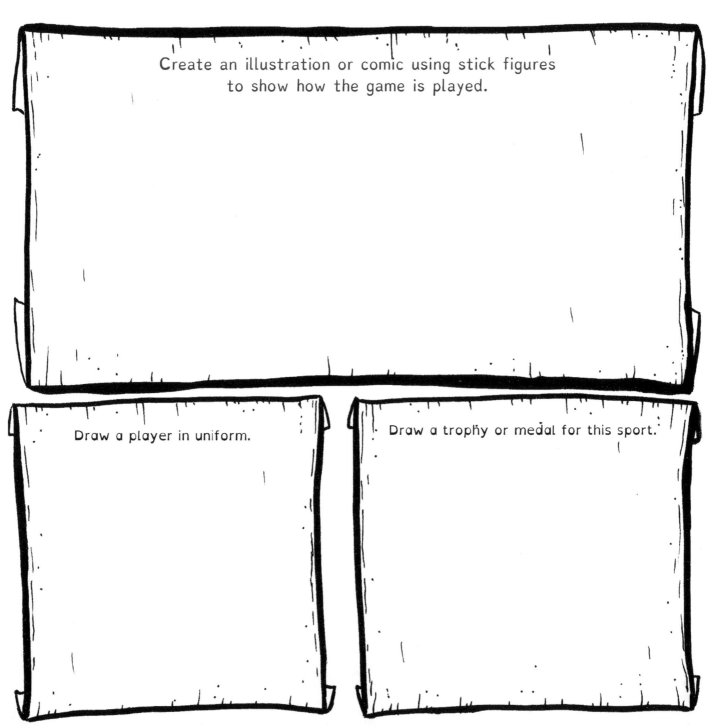

Create an illustration or comic using stick figures to show how the game is played.

Draw a player in uniform.

Draw a trophy or medal for this sport.

If you don't enjoy drawing, you may print, cut, and paste photos from the internet or a magazine onto this page.

Where did this sport originate?
_____
_____

How was this sport invented?
_____
_____
_____

Who are the main sponsors of the events for this sport?
_____
_____

What is the name of the largest competition where this sport is played? _____
_____
_____
_____
_____

Who is the #1 player of this sport? What makes them the best? How much money do they earn? Where do their earnings come from?
_____
_____
_____
_____

Would you like to play this sport? Why or why not?
_____
_____

What are the common injuries from playing this sport?
_____
_____
_____

What is a random fact about this sport?
_____
_____
_____

Canoe/Kayak Flatwater

Who were the winners in the most recent Olympics?

Medal	Men's Competition	Score	Women's Competition	Score
Gold				
Silver				
Bronze				

Research Challenge

Canoe/Kayak Flat Water
What are the distances for each of the
Canoe/Kayak Flatwater courses?

Design Challenge

Design a competition area, playing field, equipment,
or score board for this sport:

Sport Study
Canoe/Kayak Flatwater

It's research time!
Use the Internet, books, tutorials and documentaries to study this sport. Or go see a game or competition!

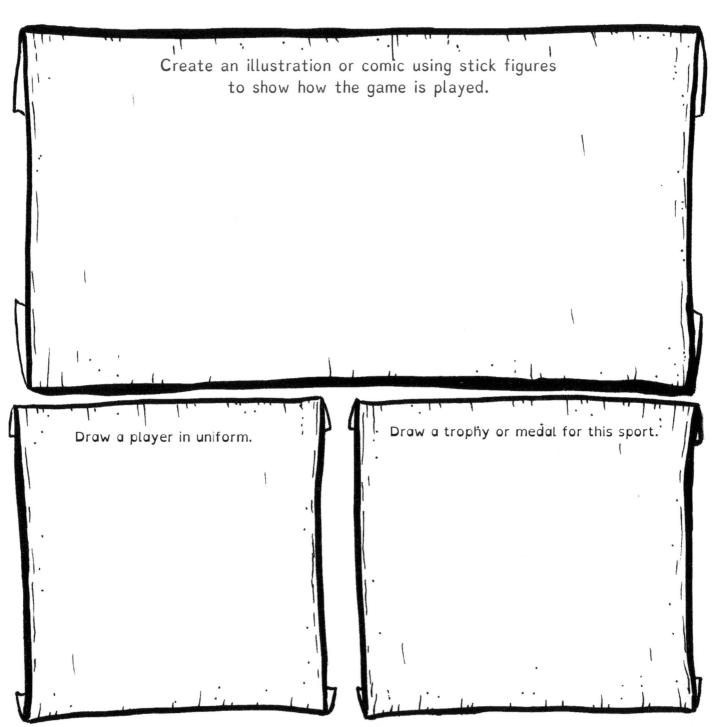

Create an illustration or comic using stick figures to show how the game is played.

Draw a player in uniform.

Draw a trophy or medal for this sport.

If you don't enjoy drawing, you may print, cut, and paste photos from the internet or a magazine onto this page.

Where did this sport originate?
_____
_____

How was this sport invented?
_____
_____
_____

Who are the main sponsors of the events for this sport?
_____
_____

What is the name of the largest competition where this sport is played? _____
_____
_____
_____
_____
_____

Who is the #1 player of this sport? What makes them the best? How much money do they earn? Where do their earnings come from?
_____
_____
_____
_____

Would you like to play this sport? Why or why not?
_____
_____

What are the common injuries from playing this sport?
_____
_____
_____

What is a random fact about this sport?
_____
_____
_____

Canoe/Kayak Slalom

Who were the winners in the most recent Olympics?

Medal	Men's Competition	Score	Women's Competition	Score
Gold				
Silver				
Bronze				

Research Challenge

Canoe/Kayak Slalom
What is the difference between Canoe and Kayak Slalom?

Design Challenge

Design a competition area, playing field, equipment, or score board for this sport:

Sport Study
Canoe/Kayak Slalom

It's research time!
Use the Internet, books, tutorials and documentaries to study this sport. Or go see a game or competition!

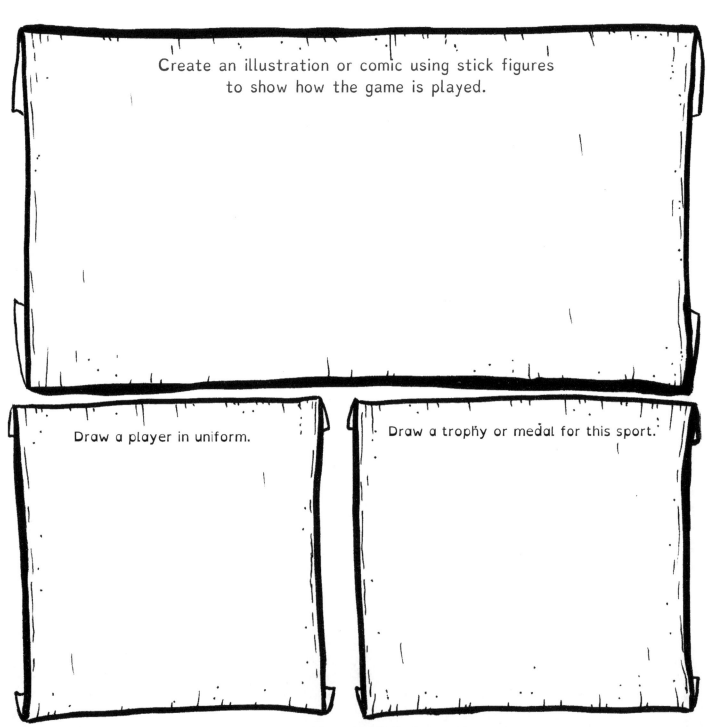

Create an illustration or comic using stick figures to show how the game is played.

Draw a player in uniform.

Draw a trophy or medal for this sport.

If you don't enjoy drawing, you may print, cut, and paste photos from the internet or a magazine onto this page.

Where did this sport originate?
_____
_____

How was this sport invented?
_____
_____
_____

Who are the main sponsors of the events for this sport?
_____
_____

What is the name of the largest competition where this sport is played? _____
_____
_____
_____
_____

Who is the #1 player of this sport? What makes them the best? How much money do they earn? Where do their earnings come from?
_____
_____
_____
_____

Would you like to play this sport? Why or why not?
_____
_____

What are the common injuries from playing this sport?
_____
_____
_____

What is a random fact about this sport?
_____
_____
_____

Curling

Who were the winners in the most recent Olympics?

Medal	Men's Competition	Score	Women's Competition	Score
Gold				
Silver				
Bronze				

Research Challenge

Curling
What are the different parts of a Curling sheet?

Design Challenge

Design a competition area, playing field, equipment, or score board for this sport:

Sport Study
Curling

It's research time!
Use the Internet, books, tutorials and documentaries to study this sport. Or go see a game or competition!

Create an illustration or comic using stick figures to show how the game is played.

Draw a player in uniform.

Draw a trophy or medal for this sport.

If you don't enjoy drawing, you may print, cut, and paste photos from the internet or a magazine onto this page.

Where did this sport originate?
_____
_____

How was this sport invented?
_____
_____
_____

Who are the main sponsors of the events for this sport?
_____
_____
_____

What is the name of the largest competition where this sport is played? _____
_____
_____
_____
_____
_____

Who is the #1 player of this sport? What makes them the best? How much money do they earn? Where do their earnings come from?
_____
_____
_____
_____

Would you like to play this sport? Why or why not?
_____
_____

What are the common injuries from playing this sport?
_____
_____
_____

What is a random fact about this sport?
_____
_____
_____

Diving

Who were the winners in the most recent Olympics?

Medal	Men's Competition	Score	Women's Competition	Score
Gold				
Silver				
Bronze				

Research Challenge

Diving

How many different events are included at the Olympic Diving competitions? What are they?

Design Challenge

Design a competition area, playing field, equipment, or score board for this sport:

Sport Study
Diving

It's research time!
Use the Internet, books, tutorials and documentaries to study this sport. Or go see a game or competition!

Create an illustration or comic using stick figures to show how the game is played.

Draw a player in uniform.

Draw a trophy or medal for this sport.

If you don't enjoy drawing, you may print, cut, and paste photos from the internet or a magazine onto this page.

Where did this sport originate?
_____
_____

How was this sport invented?
_____
_____
_____

Who are the main sponsors of the events for this sport?
_____
_____
_____

What is the name of the largest competition where this sport is played? _____
_____
_____
_____
_____

Who is the #1 player of this sport? What makes them the best? How much money do they earn? Where do their earnings come from?
_____
_____
_____
_____

Would you like to play this sport? Why or why not?
_____
_____

What are the common injuries from playing this sport?
_____
_____
_____

What is a random fact about this sport?
_____
_____
_____

Fencing

Who were the winners in the most recent Olympics?

Medal	Men's Competition	Score	Women's Competition	Score
Gold				
Silver				
Bronze				

Research Challenge

Fencing
What are 3 types of Olympic Fencing?
Give a brief description of each.

_____
_____
_____
_____
_____
_____
_____
_____

Design Challenge

Design a competition area, playing field, equipment, or score board for this sport:

Sport Study
Fencing

It's research time!
Use the Internet, books, tutorials and documentaries to study this sport. Or go see a game or competition!

Create an illustration or comic using stick figures to show how the game is played.

Draw a player in uniform.

Draw a trophy or medal for this sport.

If you don't enjoy drawing, you may print, cut, and paste photos from the internet or a magazine onto this page.

Where did this sport originate?
_____
_____

How was this sport invented?
_____
_____
_____

Who are the main sponsors of the events for this sport?
_____
_____

What is the name of the largest competition where this sport is played? _____
_____
_____
_____
_____

Who is the #1 player of this sport? What makes them the best? How much money do they earn? Where do their earnings come from?
_____
_____
_____
_____

Would you like to play this sport? Why or why not?
_____
_____

What are the common injuries from playing this sport?
_____
_____
_____

What is a random fact about this sport?
_____
_____
_____

Figure Skating

There are additional pages in this section for multiple types of figure skating competitions.

Who were the winners in the most recent Olympics?

Medal	Men's Competition	Score	Women's Competition	Score
Gold				
Silver				
Bronze				

Research Challenge

Figure Skating
What are the different medaled events for Figure Skating?

Design Challenge

Design a competition area, playing field, equipment, or score board for this sport:

Figure Skating (Pairs)

Who were winners in the most recent Olympics?

Medal	Men's Competition	Score	Women's Competition	Score
Gold				
Silver				
Bronze				

Figure Skating (Dance)

Draw your own illustration or cut and paste and image here:

Who were winners in the most recent Olympics?

Medal	Men's Competition	Score	Women's Competition	Score
Gold				
Silver				
Bronze				

Sport Study
Figure Skating

It's research time!
Use the Internet, books, tutorials and documentaries to study this sport. Or go see a game or competition!

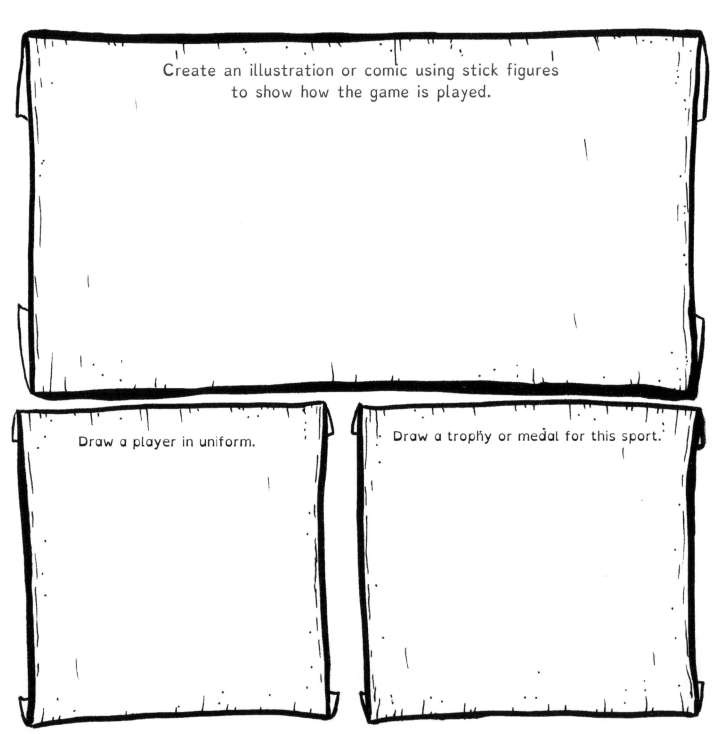

Create an illustration or comic using stick figures to show how the game is played.

Draw a player in uniform.

Draw a trophy or medal for this sport.

If you don't enjoy drawing, you may print, cut, and paste photos from the internet or a magazine onto this page.

Where did this sport originate?
_____
_____

How was this sport invented?
_____
_____
_____

Who are the main sponsors of the events for this sport?
_____
_____

What is the name of the largest competition where this sport is played? _____
_____
_____
_____
_____

Who is the #1 player of this sport? What makes them the best? How much money do they earn? Where do their earnings come from?
_____
_____
_____
_____

Would you like to play this sport? Why or why not?
_____
_____

What are the common injuries from playing this sport?
_____
_____
_____

What is a random fact about this sport?
_____
_____
_____

Football (Soccer)

Who were the winners in the most recent Olympics?

Medal	Men's Competition	Score	Women's Competition	Score
Gold				
Silver				
Bronze				

Research Challenge

Football (Soccer)
What is the maximum age of male competitors
and are there any exceptions?

Design Challenge

Design a competition area, playing field, equipment,
or score board for this sport:

Sport Study
Football (Soccer)

It's research time!
Use the Internet, books, tutorials and documentaries to study this sport. Or go see a game or competition!

Create an illustration or comic using stick figures to show how the game is played.

Draw a player in uniform.

Draw a trophy or medal for this sport.

If you don't enjoy drawing, you may print, cut, and paste photos from the internet or a magazine onto this page.

Where did this sport originate?
_____
_____

How was this sport invented?
_____
_____
_____

Who are the main sponsors of the events for this sport?
_____
_____

What is the name of the largest competition where this sport is played? _____
_____
_____
_____
_____

Who is the #1 player of this sport? What makes them the best? How much money do they earn? Where do their earnings come from?
_____
_____
_____
_____

Would you like to play this sport? Why or why not?
_____
_____

What are the common injuries from playing this sport?
_____
_____
_____

What is a random fact about this sport?
_____
_____
_____

Freestyle Skiing

Who were the winners in the most recent Olympics?

Medal	Men's Competition	Score	Women's Competition	Score
Gold				
Silver				
Bronze				

Research Challenge

Freestyle Skiing
What are the six different events that make up Olympic Freestyle Skiing? Which do you think requires the most skill?

_____
_____
_____
_____
_____
_____
_____

Design Challenge

Design a competition area, playing field, equipment, or score board for this sport:

Sport Study
Freestyle Skiing

It's research time!
Use the Internet, books, tutorials and documentaries to study this sport. Or go see a game or competition!

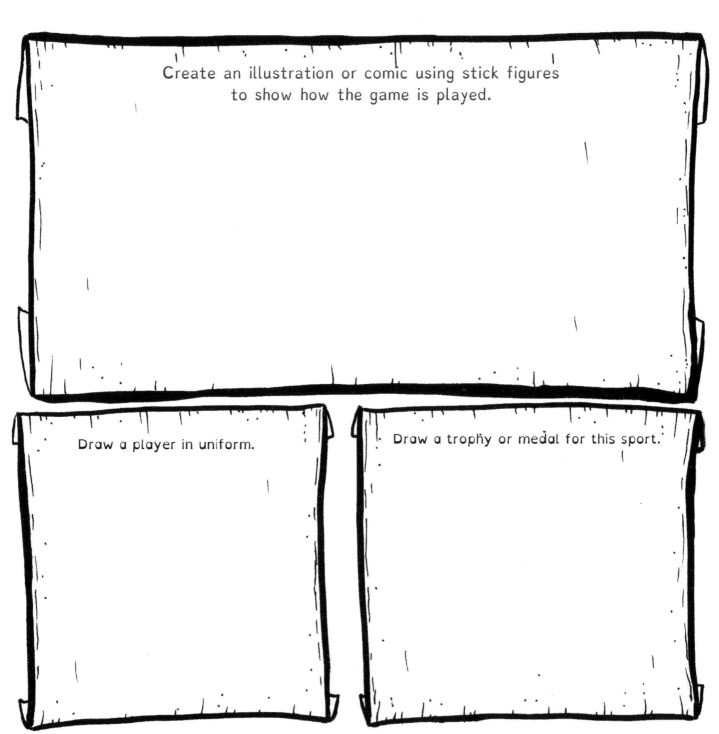

Create an illustration or comic using stick figures to show how the game is played.

Draw a player in uniform.

Draw a trophy or medal for this sport.

If you don't enjoy drawing, you may print, cut, and paste photos from the internet or a magazine onto this page.

Where did this sport originate?
_____
_____

How was this sport invented?
_____
_____
_____

Who are the main sponsors of the events for this sport?
_____
_____

What is the name of the largest competition where this sport is played? _____
_____
_____
_____
_____

Who is the #1 player of this sport? What makes them the best? How much money do they earn? Where do their earnings come from?
_____
_____
_____
_____

Would you like to play this sport? Why or why not?
_____
_____

What are the common injuries from playing this sport?
_____
_____
_____

What is a random fact about this sport?
_____
_____
_____

Futsal

Who were the winners in the most recent Olympics?

Medal	Men's Competition	Score	Women's Competition	Score
Gold				
Silver				
Bronze				

Research Challenge

Futsal
How is Futsal different from Football/Soccer?

_____
_____
_____
_____
_____
_____

Design Challenge

Design a competition area, playing field, equipment, or score board for this sport:

Sport Study
Futsal

It's research time!
Use the Internet, books, tutorials and documentaries to study this sport. Or go see a game or competition!

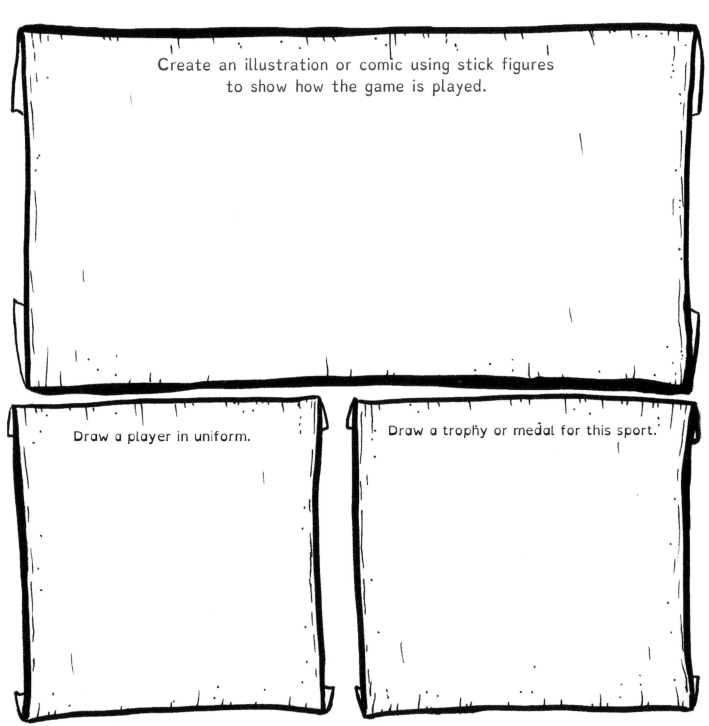

Create an illustration or comic using stick figures to show how the game is played.

Draw a player in uniform.

Draw a trophy or medal for this sport.

If you don't enjoy drawing, you may print, cut, and paste photos from the internet or a magazine onto this page.

Where did this sport originate?
_____
_____

How was this sport invented?
_____
_____
_____

Who are the main sponsors of the events for this sport?
_____
_____

What is the name of the largest competition where this sport is played? _____
_____
_____
_____
_____
_____

Who is the #1 player of this sport? What makes them the best? How much money do they earn? Where do their earnings come from?
_____
_____
_____
_____

Would you like to play this sport? Why or why not?
_____
_____

What are the common injuries from playing this sport?
_____
_____
_____

What is a random fact about this sport?
_____
_____
_____

Golf

Who were the winners in the most recent Olympics?

Medal	Men's Competition	Score	Women's Competition	Score
Gold				
Silver				
Bronze				

Research Challenge

Golf
How does a competitor qualify to compete in Olympic golf?

Design Challenge

Design a competition area, playing field, equipment, or score board for this sport:

Sport Study
Golf

It's research time!
Use the Internet, books, tutorials and documentaries to study this sport. Or go see a game or competition!

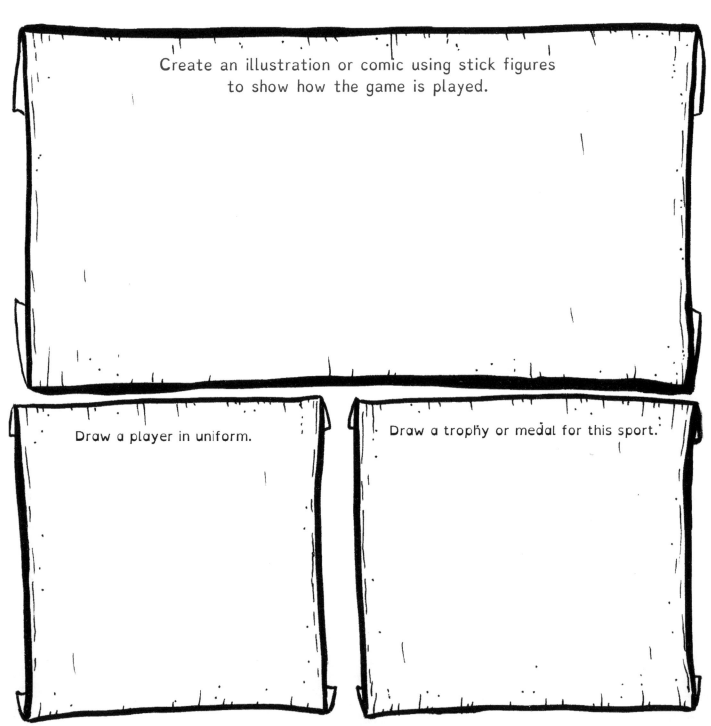

Create an illustration or comic using stick figures to show how the game is played.

Draw a player in uniform.

Draw a trophy or medal for this sport.

If you don't enjoy drawing, you may print, cut, and paste photos from the internet or a magazine onto this page.

Where did this sport originate?
_____
_____

How was this sport invented?
_____
_____
_____

Who are the main sponsors of the events for this sport?
_____
_____

What is the name of the largest competition where this sport is played? _____
_____
_____
_____
_____
_____

Who is the #1 player of this sport? What makes them the best? How much money do they earn? Where do their earnings come from?
_____
_____
_____
_____

Would you like to play this sport? Why or why not?
_____
_____

What are the common injuries from playing this sport?
_____
_____
_____
_____

What is a random fact about this sport?
_____
_____
_____
_____

Handball

Who were the winners in the most recent Olympics?

Medal	Men's Competition	Score	Women's Competition	Score
Gold				
Silver				
Bronze				

Research Challenge

Handball
How long does a Handball match last?

_____
_____
_____
_____
_____
_____
_____

Design Challenge

Design a competition area, playing field, equipment, or score board for this sport:

Sport Study
Handball

It's research time!
Use the Internet, books, tutorials and documentaries to study this sport. Or go see a game or competition!

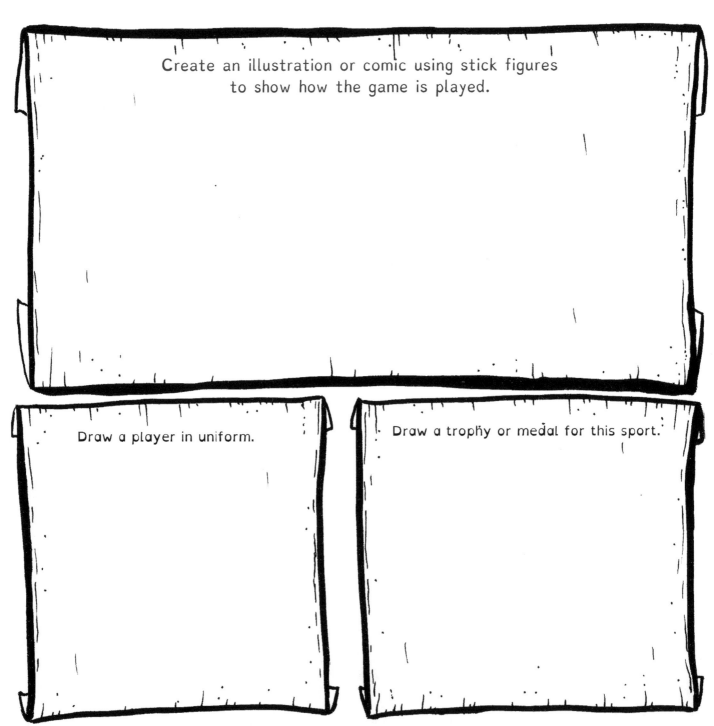

Create an illustration or comic using stick figures to show how the game is played.

Draw a player in uniform.

Draw a trophy or medal for this sport.

If you don't enjoy drawing, you may print, cut, and paste photos from the internet or a magazine onto this page.

Where did this sport originate?
_____
_____

How was this sport invented?
_____
_____
_____

Who are the main sponsors of the events for this sport?
_____
_____

What is the name of the largest competition where this sport is played? _____
_____
_____
_____
_____

Who is the #1 player of this sport? What makes them the best? How much money do they earn? Where do their earnings come from?
_____
_____
_____
_____

Would you like to play this sport? Why or why not?
_____
_____

What are the common injuries from playing this sport?
_____
_____
_____

What is a random fact about this sport?
_____
_____
_____

Hockey

Who were the winners in the most recent Olympics?

Medal	Men's Competition	Score	Women's Competition	Score
Gold				
Silver				
Bronze				

Research Challenge

Hockey

What are the two styles of Hockey played in the Olympics and when are they played?

_____
_____
_____
_____
_____
_____
_____

Design Challenge

Design a competition area, playing field, equipment, or score board for this sport:

Sport Study
Hockey

It's research time!
Use the Internet, books, tutorials and documentaries to study this sport. Or go see a game or competition!

Create an illustration or comic using stick figures to show how the game is played.

Draw a player in uniform.

Draw a trophy or medal for this sport.

If you don't enjoy drawing, you may print, cut, and paste photos from the internet or a magazine onto this page.

Where did this sport originate?
_____
_____

How was this sport invented?
_____
_____
_____
_____

Who are the main sponsors of the events for this sport?
_____
_____
_____

What is the name of the largest competition where this sport is played? _____
_____
_____
_____
_____
_____

Who is the #1 player of this sport? What makes them the best? How much money do they earn? Where do their earnings come from?
_____
_____
_____
_____
_____

Would you like to play this sport? Why or why not?
_____
_____

What are the common injuries from playing this sport?
_____
_____
_____
_____

What is a random fact about this sport?
_____
_____
_____
_____

Karate

Who were the winners in the most recent Olympics?

Medal	Men's Competition	Score	Women's Competition	Score
Gold				
Silver				
Bronze				

Research Challenge

Karate
What are the two types of Karate that are used in the Olympics and how many competitors are on the mat for each?

_____
_____
_____
_____
_____
_____

Design Challenge

Design a competition area, playing field, equipment, or score board for this sport:

Sport Study
Karate

It's research time!
Use the Internet, books, tutorials and documentaries to study this sport. Or go see a game or competition!

Create an illustration or comic using stick figures to show how the game is played.

Draw a player in uniform.

Draw a trophy or medal for this sport.

If you don't enjoy drawing, you may print, cut, and paste photos from the internet or a magazine onto this page.

Where did this sport originate?
_____
_____

How was this sport invented?
_____
_____
_____

Who are the main sponsors of the events for this sport?
_____
_____

What is the name of the largest competition where this sport is played? _____
_____
_____
_____
_____

Who is the #1 player of this sport? What makes them the best? How much money do they earn? Where do their earnings come from?
_____
_____
_____
_____

Would you like to play this sport? Why or why not?
_____
_____

What are the common injuries from playing this sport?
_____
_____
_____

What is a random fact about this sport?
_____
_____
_____

Luge

Who were the winners in the most recent Olympics?

Medal	Men's Competition	Score	Women's Competition	Score
Gold				
Silver				
Bronze				

Research Challenge

Luge
What are the 4 different Luge disciplines?

_____
_____
_____
_____
_____
_____
_____

Design Challenge

Design a competition area, playing field, equipment, or score board for this sport:

Sport Study
Luge

It's research time!
Use the Internet, books, tutorials and documentaries to study this sport. Or go see a game or competition!

Create an illustration or comic using stick figures to show how the game is played.

Draw a player in uniform.

Draw a trophy or medal for this sport.

If you don't enjoy drawing, you may print, cut, and paste photos from the internet or a magazine onto this page.

Where did this sport originate?
_____
_____

How was this sport invented?
_____
_____
_____

Who are the main sponsors of the events for this sport?
_____
_____

What is the name of the largest competition where this sport is played? _____
_____
_____
_____
_____

Who is the #1 player of this sport? What makes them the best? How much money do they earn? Where do their earnings come from?
_____
_____
_____
_____

Would you like to play this sport? Why or why not?
_____
_____

What are the common injuries from playing this sport?
_____
_____
_____

What is a random fact about this sport?
_____
_____
_____

Marathon Swimming

Who were the winners in the most recent Olympics?

Medal	Men's Competition	Score	Women's Competition	Score
Gold				
Silver				
Bronze				

Research Challenge

Marathon Swimming
What is the minimum distance for the Marathon Swimming event in the Olympics and approximately how long does it take?

_____
_____
_____
_____
_____
_____
_____

Design Challenge

Design a competition area, playing field, equipment, or score board for this sport:

Sport Study
Marathon Swimming

It's research time!
Use the Internet, books, tutorials and documentaries to study this sport. Or go see a game or competition!

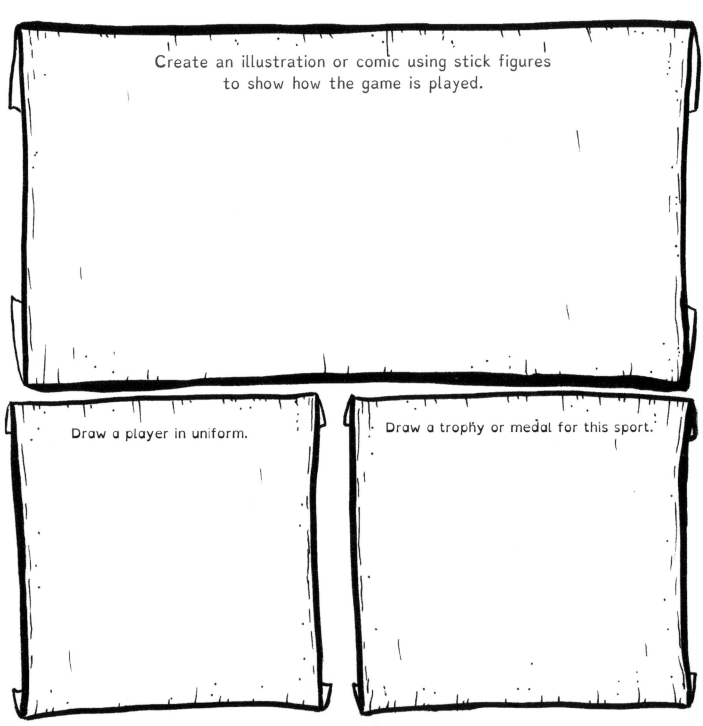

Create an illustration or comic using stick figures to show how the game is played.

Draw a player in uniform.

Draw a trophy or medal for this sport.

If you don't enjoy drawing, you may print, cut, and paste photos from the internet or a magazine onto this page.

Where did this sport originate?
_____
_____

How was this sport invented?
_____
_____
_____

Who are the main sponsors of the events for this sport?
_____
_____
_____

What is the name of the largest competition where this sport is played? _____
_____
_____
_____
_____
_____

Who is the #1 player of this sport? What makes them the best? How much money do they earn? Where do their earnings come from?
_____
_____
_____
_____
_____

Would you like to play this sport? Why or why not?
_____
_____

What are the common injuries from playing this sport?
_____
_____
_____

What is a random fact about this sport?
_____
_____
_____

Modern Pentathlon

Who were the winners in the most recent Olympics?

Medal	Men's Competition	Score	Women's Competition	Score
Gold				
Silver				
Bronze				

Research Challenge

Modern Pentathlon
What are the 5 different events that make up the Modern Pentathlon?

_____
_____
_____
_____
_____
_____
_____

Design Challenge

Design a competition area, playing field, equipment, or score board for this sport:

Sport Study
Modern Pentathlon

It's research time!
Use the Internet, books, tutorials and documentaries to study this sport. Or go see a game or competition!

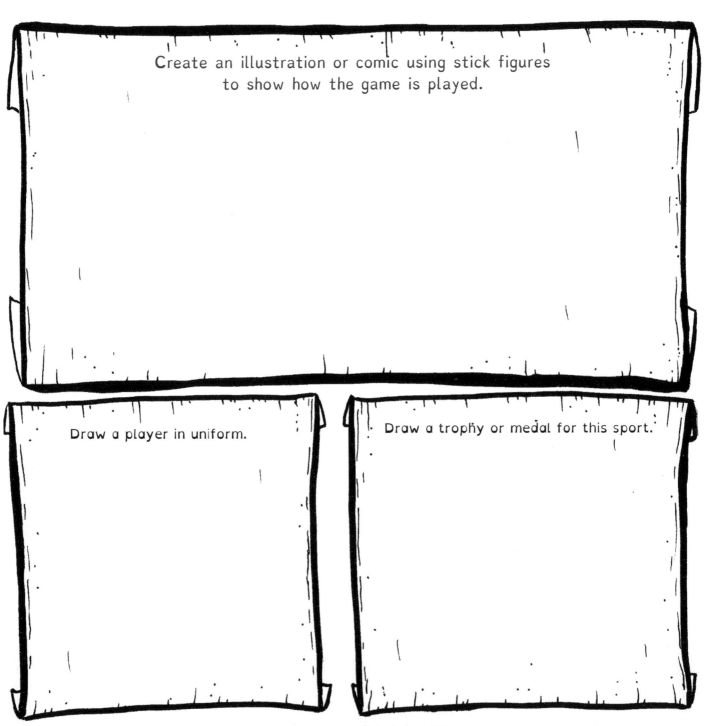

Create an illustration or comic using stick figures to show how the game is played.

Draw a player in uniform.

Draw a trophy or medal for this sport.

If you don't enjoy drawing, you may print, cut, and paste photos from the internet or a magazine onto this page.

Where did this sport originate?
_____
_____

How was this sport invented?
_____
_____
_____

Who are the main sponsors of the events for this sport?
_____
_____

What is the name of the largest competition where this sport is played? _____
_____
_____
_____
_____

Who is the #1 player of this sport? What makes them the best? How much money do they earn? Where do their earnings come from?
_____
_____
_____
_____

Would you like to play this sport? Why or why not?
_____
_____

What are the common injuries from playing this sport?
_____
_____
_____

What is a random fact about this sport?
_____
_____
_____

Mountain Bike

Who were the winners in the most recent Olympics?

Medal	Men's Competition	Score	Women's Competition	Score
Gold				
Silver				
Bronze				

Research Challenge

Mountain Bike

What are some special features of mountain bikes that differ from other bikes to make them able to perform better on rough terrain?

_____
_____
_____
_____
_____
_____

Design Challenge

Design a competition area, playing field, equipment, or score board for this sport:

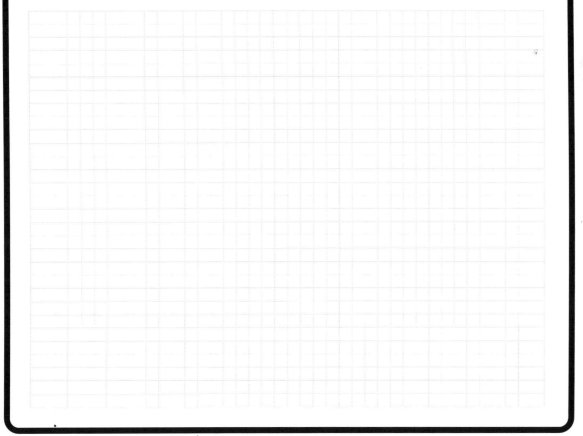

Sport Study
Mountain Bike

It's research time!
Use the Internet, books, tutorials and documentaries to study this sport. Or go see a game or competition!

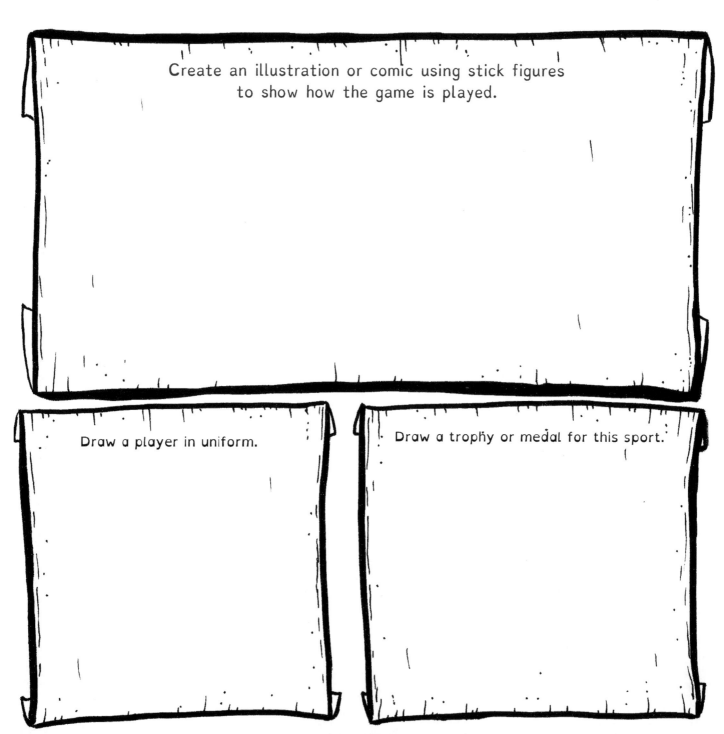

Create an illustration or comic using stick figures to show how the game is played.

Draw a player in uniform.

Draw a trophy or medal for this sport.

If you don't enjoy drawing, you may print, cut, and paste photos from the internet or a magazine onto this page.

Where did this sport originate?
_____
_____

How was this sport invented?
_____
_____
_____

Who are the main sponsors of the events for this sport?
_____
_____

What is the name of the largest competition where this sport is played? _____
_____
_____
_____
_____

Who is the #1 player of this sport? What makes them the best? How much money do they earn? Where do their earnings come from?
_____
_____
_____
_____

Would you like to play this sport? Why or why not?
_____
_____

What are the common injuries from playing this sport?
_____
_____
_____

What is a random fact about this sport?
_____
_____
_____

Nordic Combined

Who were the winners in the most recent Olympics?

Medal	Men's Competition	Score	Women's Competition	Score
Gold				
Silver				
Bronze				

Research Challenge

Nordic Combined
Nordic Combined is a mixture of which two sports?

_____
_____
_____
_____
_____
_____

Design Challenge

Design a competition area, playing field, equipment, or score board for this sport:

Sport Study
Nordic Combined

It's research time!
Use the Internet, books, tutorials and documentaries to study this sport. Or go see a game or competition!

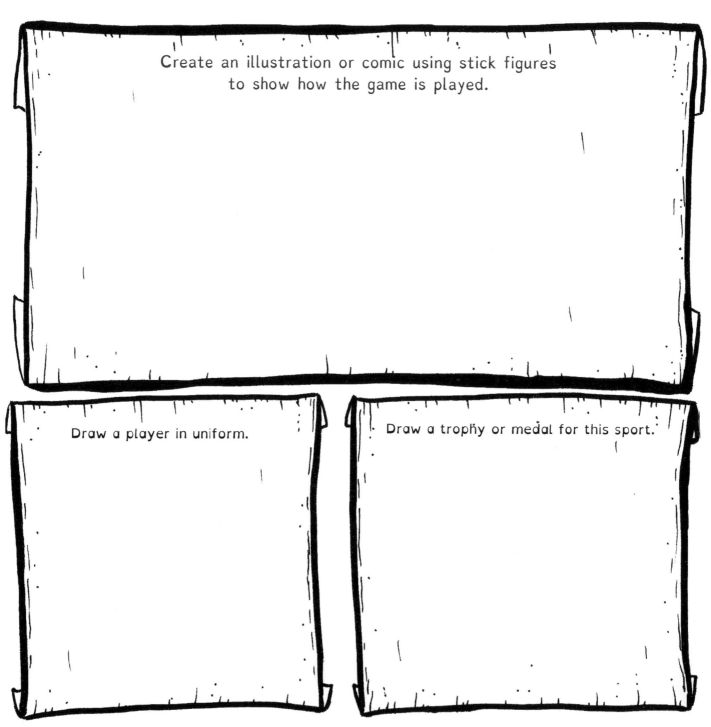

Create an illustration or comic using stick figures to show how the game is played.

Draw a player in uniform.

Draw a trophy or medal for this sport.

If you don't enjoy drawing, you may print, cut, and paste photos from the internet or a magazine onto this page.

Where did this sport originate?
_____
_____

How was this sport invented?
_____
_____
_____

Who are the main sponsors of the events for this sport?
_____
_____

What is the name of the largest competition where this sport is played? _____
_____
_____
_____
_____

Who is the #1 player of this sport? What makes them the best? How much money do they earn? Where do their earnings come from?
_____
_____
_____

Would you like to play this sport? Why or why not?
_____
_____

What are the common injuries from playing this sport?
_____
_____
_____

What is a random fact about this sport?
_____
_____
_____

Rhythmic Gymnastics

Who were the winners in the most recent Olympics?

Medal	Men's Competition	Score	Women's Competition	Score
Gold				
Silver				
Bronze				

Research Challenge

Rhythmic Gymnastics
What 5 items are used in Rhythmic Gymnastics?

Design Challenge

Design a competition area, playing field, equipment, or score board for this sport:

Sport Study
Rhythmic Gymnastics

It's research time!
Use the Internet, books, tutorials and documentaries to study this sport. Or go see a game or competition!

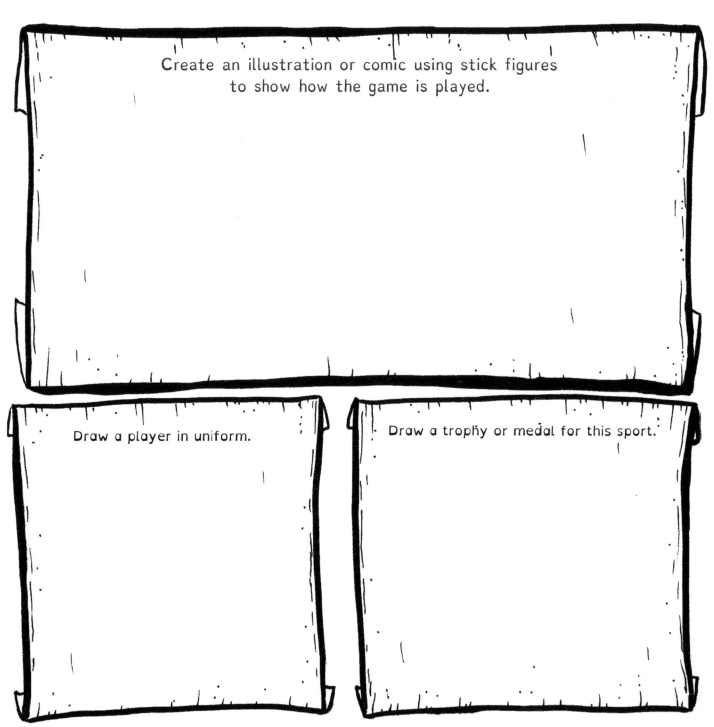

Create an illustration or comic using stick figures to show how the game is played.

Draw a player in uniform.

Draw a trophy or medal for this sport.

If you don't enjoy drawing, you may print, cut, and paste photos from the internet or a magazine onto this page.

Where did this sport originate?
_____
_____

How was this sport invented?
_____
_____
_____

Who are the main sponsors of the events for this sport?
_____
_____
_____

What is the name of the largest competition where this sport is played? _____
_____
_____
_____
_____

Who is the #1 player of this sport? What makes them the best? How much money do they earn? Where do their earnings come from?
_____
_____
_____
_____

Would you like to play this sport? Why or why not?
_____
_____

What are the common injuries from playing this sport?
_____
_____
_____

What is a random fact about this sport?
_____
_____
_____

Roller Speed Skating

Who were the winners in the most recent Olympics?

Medal	Men's Competition	Score	Women's Competition	Score
Gold				
Silver				
Bronze				

Research Challenge

Roller Speed Skating
What is the average speed in Roller Speed Skating?

Design Challenge

Design a competition area, playing field, equipment, or score board for this sport:

Sport Study
Roller Speed Skating

It's research time!
Use the Internet, books, tutorials and documentaries to study this sport. Or go see a game or competition!

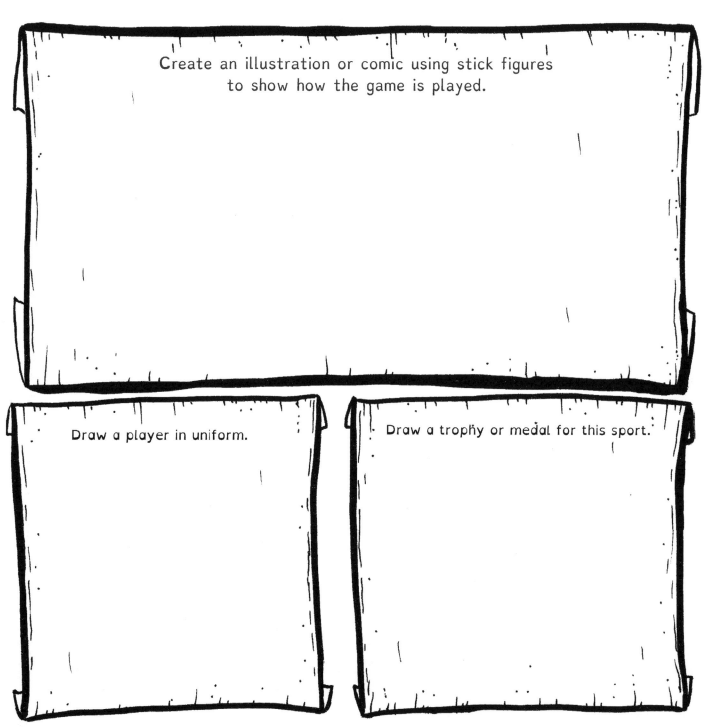

Create an illustration or comic using stick figures to show how the game is played.

Draw a player in uniform.

Draw a trophy or medal for this sport.

If you don't enjoy drawing, you may print, cut, and paste photos from the internet or a magazine onto this page.

Where did this sport originate?
_____
_____

How was this sport invented?
_____
_____
_____

Who are the main sponsors of the events for this sport?
_____
_____

What is the name of the largest competition where this sport is played? _____
_____
_____
_____
_____

Who is the #1 player of this sport? What makes them the best? How much money do they earn? Where do their earnings come from?
_____
_____
_____
_____

Would you like to play this sport? Why or why not?
_____
_____

What are the common injuries from playing this sport?
_____
_____
_____

What is a random fact about this sport?
_____
_____
_____

Rowing

Who were the winners in the most recent Olympics?

Medal	Men's Competition	Score	Women's Competition	Score
Gold				
Silver				
Bronze				

Research Challenge

Rowing
How many oars are used in each of the two
following types of Rowing- Sweep Rowing and Sculling?

_____
_____
_____
_____
_____
_____

Design Challenge

Design a competition area, playing field, equipment,
or score board for this sport:

Sport Study
Rowing

It's research time!
Use the Internet, books, tutorials and documentaries to study this sport. Or go see a game or competition!

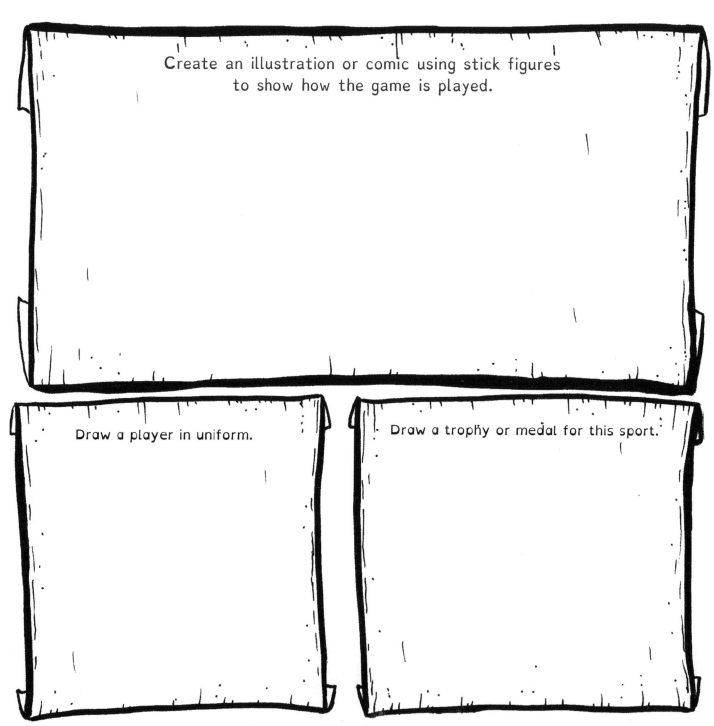

Create an illustration or comic using stick figures to show how the game is played.

Draw a player in uniform.

Draw a trophy or medal for this sport.

If you don't enjoy drawing, you may print, cut, and paste photos from the internet or a magazine onto this page.

Where did this sport originate?
_____
_____

How was this sport invented?
_____
_____
_____

Who are the main sponsors of the events for this sport?
_____
_____

What is the name of the largest competition where this sport is played? _____
_____
_____
_____
_____

Who is the #1 player of this sport? What makes them the best? How much money do they earn? Where do their earnings come from?
_____
_____
_____
_____

Would you like to play this sport? Why or why not?
_____
_____

What are the common injuries from playing this sport?
_____
_____
_____

What is a random fact about this sport?
_____
_____
_____

Rugby

Who were the winners in the most recent Olympics?

Medal	Men's Competition	Score	Women's Competition	Score
Gold				
Silver				
Bronze				

Research Challenge

Rugby
How many players and how many substitutes play in an Olympic Rugby match?

Design Challenge

Design a competition area, playing field, equipment, or score board for this sport:

Sport Study
Rugby

It's research time!
Use the Internet, books, tutorials and documentaries to study this sport. Or go see a game or competition!

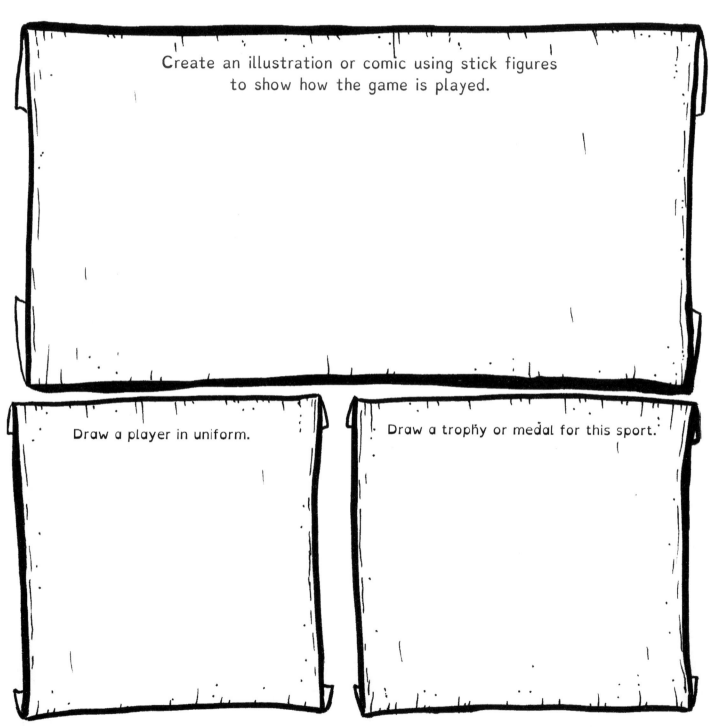

Create an illustration or comic using stick figures to show how the game is played.

Draw a player in uniform.

Draw a trophy or medal for this sport.

If you don't enjoy drawing, you may print, cut, and paste photos from the internet or a magazine onto this page.

Where did this sport originate?
_____
_____

How was this sport invented?
_____
_____
_____

Who are the main sponsors of the events for this sport?
_____
_____

What is the name of the largest competition where this sport is played? _____
_____
_____
_____
_____

Who is the #1 player of this sport? What makes them the best? How much money do they earn? Where do their earnings come from?
_____
_____
_____
_____

Would you like to play this sport? Why or why not?
_____
_____

What are the common injuries from playing this sport?
_____
_____
_____

What is a random fact about this sport?
_____
_____
_____

Shooting

Who were the winners in the most recent Olympics?

Medal	Men's Competition	Score	Women's Competition	Score
Gold				
Silver				
Bronze				

Research Challenge

Shooting

How many Shooting games are included in the Olympic events?

Design Challenge

Design a competition area, playing field, equipment, or score board for this sport:

Sport Study
Shooting

It's research time!
Use the Internet, books, tutorials and documentaries to study this sport. Or go see a game or competition!

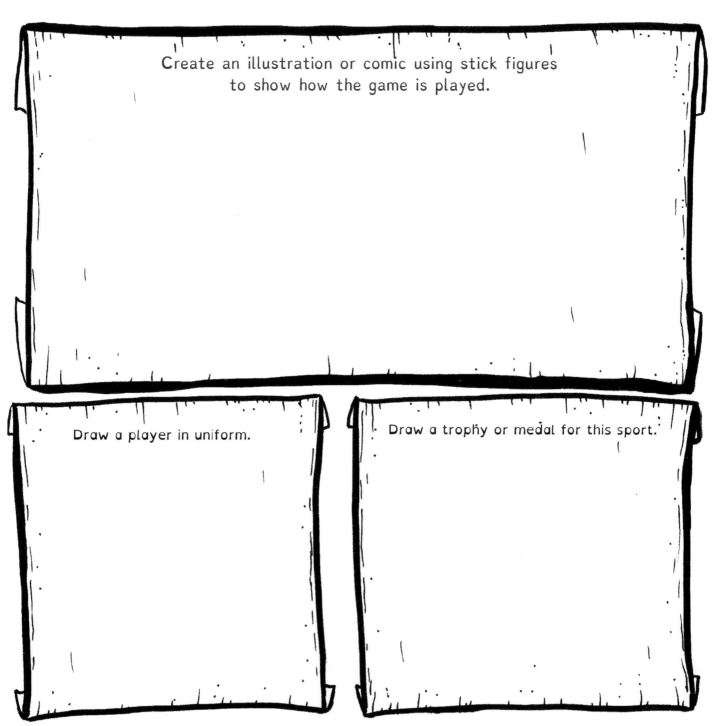

Create an illustration or comic using stick figures to show how the game is played.

Draw a player in uniform.

Draw a trophy or medal for this sport.

If you don't enjoy drawing, you may print, cut, and paste photos from the internet or a magazine onto this page.

Where did this sport originate?
_____
_____

How was this sport invented?
_____
_____
_____

Who are the main sponsors of the events for this sport?
_____
_____

What is the name of the largest competition where this sport is played? _____
_____
_____
_____
_____

Who is the #1 player of this sport? What makes them the best? How much money do they earn? Where do their earnings come from?
_____
_____
_____

Would you like to play this sport? Why or why not?
_____
_____

What are the common injuries from playing this sport?
_____
_____
_____

What is a random fact about this sport?
_____
_____
_____

Short Track Speed Skating

Who were the winners in the most recent Olympics?

Medal	Men's Competition	Score	Women's Competition	Score
Gold				
Silver				
Bronze				

Research Challenge

Short Track Speed Skating

In Short Track Speed Skating what does the term "Impeding" mean?

_____
_____
_____
_____
_____
_____

Design Challenge

Design a competition area, playing field, equipment, or score board for this sport:

Sport Study
Short Track Speed Skating

It's research time!
Use the Internet, books, tutorials and documentaries to study this sport. Or go see a game or competition!

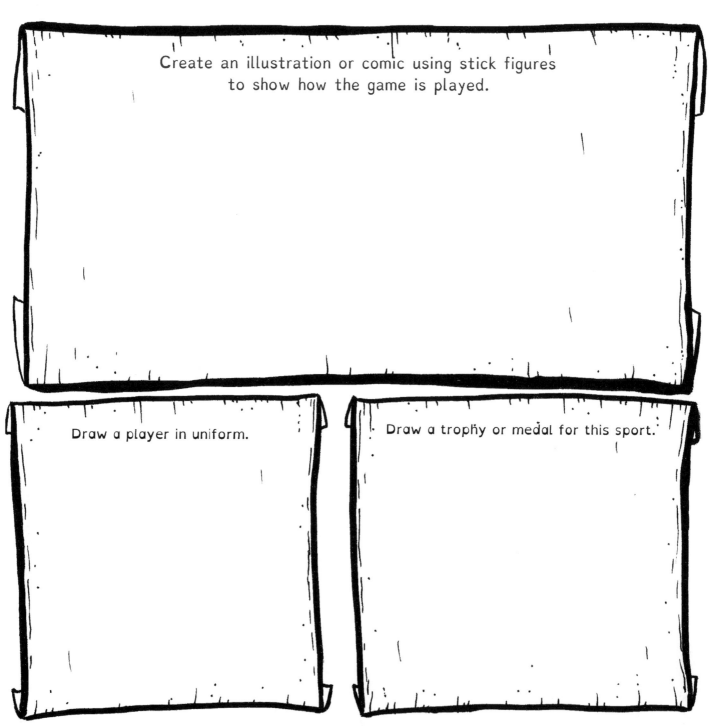

Create an illustration or comic using stick figures to show how the game is played.

Draw a player in uniform.

Draw a trophy or medal for this sport.

If you don't enjoy drawing, you may print, cut, and paste photos from the internet or a magazine onto this page.

Where did this sport originate?
_____
_____

How was this sport invented?
_____
_____
_____

Who are the main sponsors of the events for this sport?
_____
_____

What is the name of the largest competition where this sport is played? _____
_____
_____
_____
_____

Who is the #1 player of this sport? What makes them the best? How much money do they earn? Where do their earnings come from?
_____
_____
_____
_____

Would you like to play this sport? Why or why not?
_____
_____

What are the common injuries from playing this sport?
_____
_____
_____

What is a random fact about this sport?
_____
_____
_____

Skateboarding

Who were the winners in the most recent Olympics?

Medal	Men's Competition	Score	Women's Competition	Score
Gold				
Silver				
Bronze				

Research Challenge

Skateboarding
Are Olympic participants required to wear helmets during skateboarding competitions? Do you agree with this? Why or why not?

_____
_____
_____
_____
_____
_____

Design Challenge

Design a competition area, playing field, equipment, or score board for this sport:

Sport Study
Skateboarding

It's research time!
Use the Internet, books, tutorials and documentaries to study this sport. Or go see a game or competition!

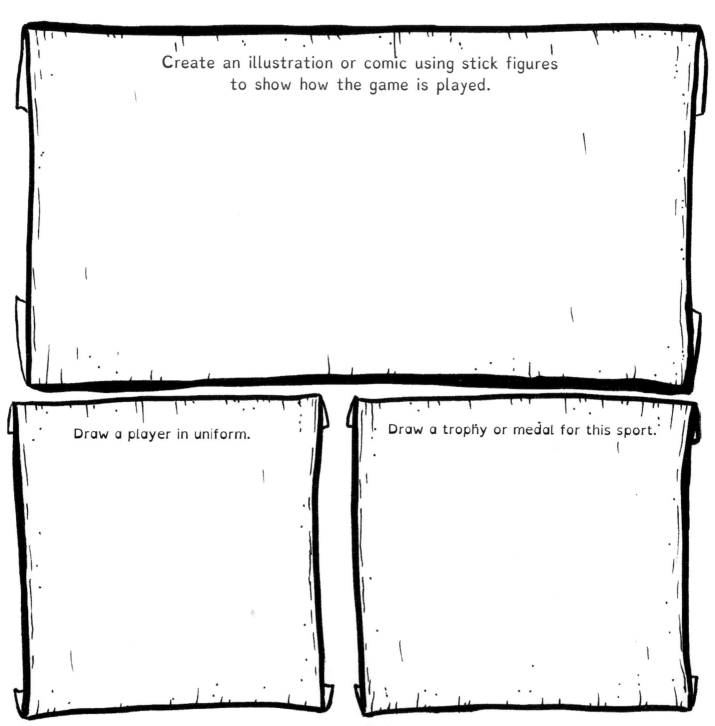

Create an illustration or comic using stick figures to show how the game is played.

Draw a player in uniform.

Draw a trophy or medal for this sport.

If you don't enjoy drawing, you may print, cut, and paste photos from the internet or a magazine onto this page.

Where did this sport originate?
_____
_____

How was this sport invented?
_____
_____
_____

Who are the main sponsors of the events for this sport?
_____
_____

What is the name of the largest competition where this sport is played? _____
_____
_____
_____
_____

Who is the #1 player of this sport? What makes them the best? How much money do they earn? Where do their earnings come from?
_____
_____
_____
_____

Would you like to play this sport? Why or why not?
_____
_____

What are the common injuries from playing this sport?
_____
_____
_____

What is a random fact about this sport?
_____
_____
_____

Skeleton

Who were the winners in the most recent Olympics?

Medal	Men's Competition	Score	Women's Competition	Score
Gold				
Silver				
Bronze				

Research Challenge

Skeleton

What is the only nation that has won a medal every time that Skeleton was a feature in the Olympic competition?

Design Challenge

Design a competition area, playing field, equipment, or score board for this sport:

Sport Study
Skeleton

It's research time!
Use the Internet, books, tutorials and documentaries to study this sport. Or go see a game or competition!

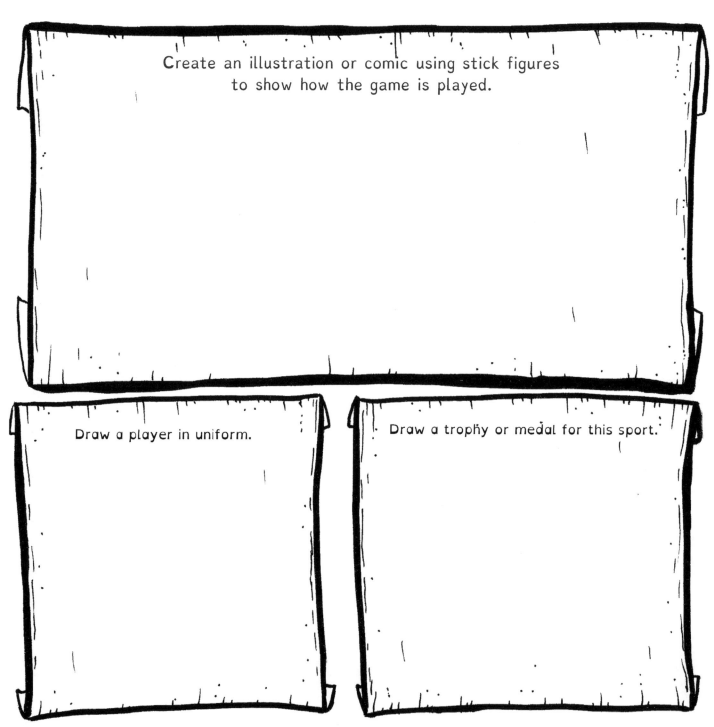

Create an illustration or comic using stick figures to show how the game is played.

Draw a player in uniform.

Draw a trophy or medal for this sport.

If you don't enjoy drawing, you may print, cut, and paste photos from the internet or a magazine onto this page.

Where did this sport originate?
_____
_____

How was this sport invented?
_____
_____
_____

Who are the main sponsors of the events for this sport?
_____
_____
_____

What is the name of the largest competition where this sport is played? _____
_____
_____
_____
_____

Who is the #1 player of this sport? What makes them the best? How much money do they earn? Where do their earnings come from?
_____
_____
_____
_____

Would you like to play this sport? Why or why not?
_____
_____

What are the common injuries from playing this sport?
_____
_____
_____

What is a random fact about this sport?
_____
_____
_____

Ski Jumping

Who were the winners in the most recent Olympics?

Medal	Men's Competition	Score	Women's Competition	Score
Gold				
Silver				
Bronze				

Research Challenge

Ski Jumping
What three parts does the Ski Jumping venue consist of?

Design Challenge

Design a competition area, playing field, equipment, or score board for this sport:

Sport Study
Ski Jumping

It's research time!
Use the Internet, books, tutorials and documentaries to study this sport. Or go see a game or competition!

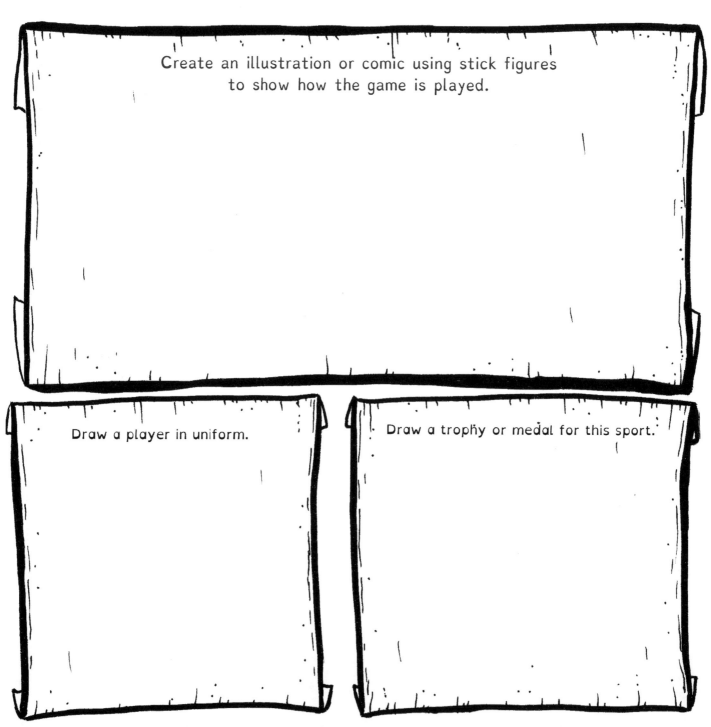

Create an illustration or comic using stick figures to show how the game is played.

Draw a player in uniform.

Draw a trophy or medal for this sport.

If you don't enjoy drawing, you may print, cut, and paste photos from the internet or a magazine onto this page.

Where did this sport originate?
_____
_____

How was this sport invented?
_____
_____
_____

Who are the main sponsors of the events for this sport?
_____
_____

What is the name of the largest competition where this sport is played? _____
_____
_____
_____
_____

Who is the #1 player of this sport? What makes them the best? How much money do they earn? Where do their earnings come from?
_____
_____
_____

Would you like to play this sport? Why or why not?
_____
_____

What are the common injuries from playing this sport?
_____
_____
_____

What is a random fact about this sport?
_____
_____
_____

Ski Mountaineering

Who were winners in the most recent Olympics?

Medal	Men's Competition	Score	Women's Competition	Score
Gold				
Silver				
Bronze				

Research Challenge

Ski Mountaineering
In July of 2021, the International Olympic Committee unanimously approved the addition of Ski Mountaineering to the 2026 Winter Olympics.

What equipment items are needed for this sport?

_____
_____
_____
_____

Design Challenge

Design a competition area, playing field, equipment, or a score board for this sport:

Sport Study
Ski Mountaineering

It's research time!
Use the Internet, books, tutorials and documentaries to study this sport. Or go see a game or competition!

Create an illustration or comic using stick figures to show how the game is played.

Draw a player in uniform.

Draw a trophy or medal for this sport.

If you don't enjoy drawing, you may print, cut, and paste photos from the internet or a magazine onto this page.

Where did this sport originate?
_____
_____

How was this sport invented?
_____
_____
_____

Who are the main sponsors of the events for this sport?
_____
_____

What is the name of the largest competition where this sport is played? _____
_____
_____
_____
_____

Who is the #1 player of this sport? What makes them the best? How much money do they earn? Where do their earnings come from?
_____
_____
_____
_____

Would you like to play this sport? Why or why not?
_____
_____

What are the common injuries from playing this sport?
_____
_____
_____

What is a random fact about this sport?
_____
_____
_____

Snowboarding

Who were the winners in the most recent Olympics?

Medal	Men's Competition	Score	Women's Competition	Score
Gold				
Silver				
Bronze				

Research Challenge

Snowboarding
Can you list all the different styles of Snowboarding?

Design Challenge

Design a competition area, playing field, equipment, or score board for this sport:

Sport Study
Snowboarding

It's research time!
Use the Internet, books, tutorials and documentaries to study this sport. Or go see a game or competition!

Create an illustration or comic using stick figures to show how the game is played.

Draw a player in uniform.

Draw a trophy or medal for this sport.

If you don't enjoy drawing, you may print, cut, and paste photos from the internet or a magazine onto this page.

Where did this sport originate?
_____
_____

How was this sport invented?
_____
_____
_____

Who are the main sponsors of the events for this sport?
_____
_____

What is the name of the largest competition where this sport is played? _____
_____
_____
_____
_____

Who is the #1 player of this sport? What makes them the best? How much money do they earn? Where do their earnings come from?
_____
_____
_____
_____

Would you like to play this sport? Why or why not?
_____
_____

What are the common injuries from playing this sport?
_____
_____
_____

What is a random fact about this sport?
_____
_____

Speed Skating

Who were the winners in the most recent Olympics?

Medal	Men's Competition	Score	Women's Competition	Score
Gold				
Silver				
Bronze				

Research Challenge

Speed Skating
What year did Speed Skating make its Olympic debut at the inaugural Winter Games at Chamonix, France?

_____
_____
_____
_____
_____
_____

Design Challenge

Design a competition area, playing field, equipment, or score board for this sport:

Sport Study
Speed Skating

It's research time!
Use the Internet, books, tutorials and documentaries to study this sport. Or go see a game or competition!

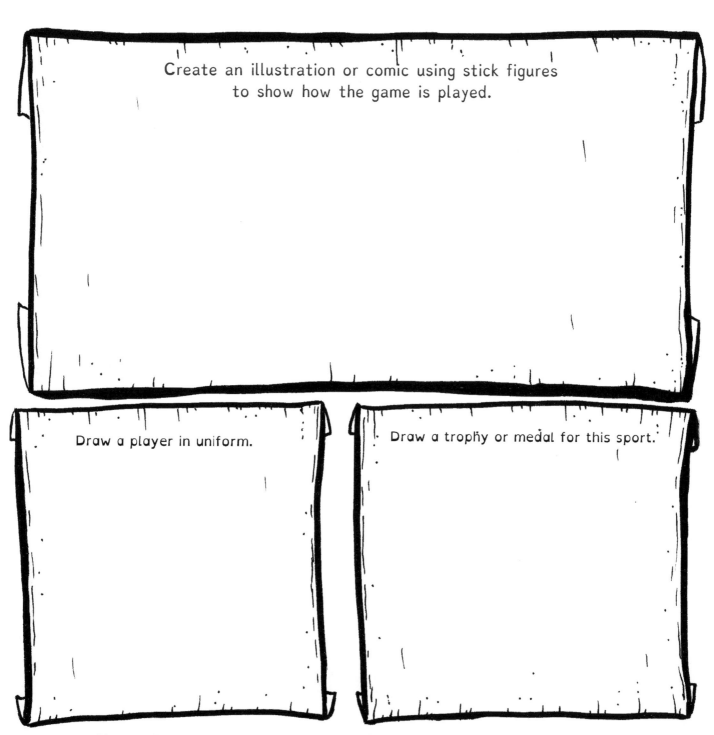

Create an illustration or comic using stick figures to show how the game is played.

Draw a player in uniform.

Draw a trophy or medal for this sport.

If you don't enjoy drawing, you may print, cut, and paste photos from the internet or a magazine onto this page.

Where did this sport originate?
_____
_____

How was this sport invented?
_____
_____
_____

Who are the main sponsors of the events for this sport?
_____
_____
_____

What is the name of the largest competition where this sport is played? _____
_____
_____
_____
_____
_____

Who is the #1 player of this sport? What makes them the best? How much money do they earn? Where do their earnings come from?
_____
_____
_____
_____

Would you like to play this sport? Why or why not?
_____
_____

What are the common injuries from playing this sport?
_____
_____
_____

What is a random fact about this sport?
_____
_____
_____

Sport Climbing

Who were the winners in the most recent Olympics?

Medal	Men's Competition	Score	Women's Competition	Score
Gold				
Silver				
Bronze				

Research Challenge

Sport Climbing
What does the Sport Climbing term "abseiling" mean?

_____
_____
_____
_____
_____
_____

Design Challenge

Design a competition area, playing field, equipment, or score board for this sport:

Sport Study
Sport Climbing

It's research time!
Use the Internet, books, tutorials and documentaries to study this sport. Or go see a game or competition!

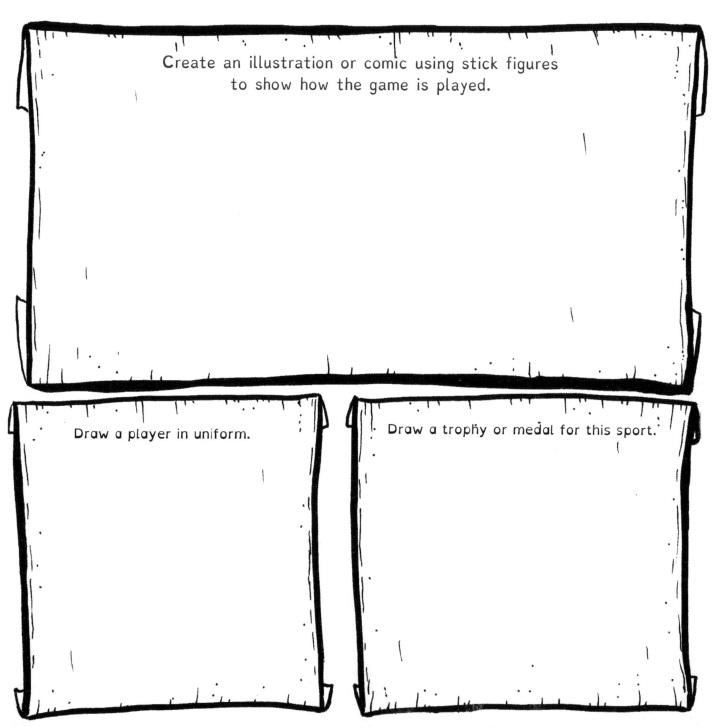

Create an illustration or comic using stick figures to show how the game is played.

Draw a player in uniform.

Draw a trophy or medal for this sport.

If you don't enjoy drawing, you may print, cut, and paste photos from the internet or a magazine onto this page.

Where did this sport originate?
_____
_____
_____

How was this sport invented?
_____
_____
_____
_____

Who are the main sponsors of the events for this sport?
_____
_____
_____

What is the name of the largest competition where this sport is played? _____
_____
_____
_____
_____
_____
_____

Who is the #1 player of this sport? What makes them the best? How much money do they earn? Where do their earnings come from?
_____
_____
_____
_____
_____

Would you like to play this sport? Why or why not?
_____
_____
_____

What are the common injuries from playing this sport?
_____
_____
_____
_____

What is a random fact about this sport?
_____
_____
_____

Surfing

Who were the winners in the most recent Olympics?

Medal	Men's Competition	Score	Women's Competition	Score
Gold				
Silver				
Bronze				

Research Challenge

Surfing
What are the three major subdivisions in Stand Up Surfing?

_____
_____
_____
_____
_____
_____
_____

Design Challenge

Design a competition area, playing field, equipment, or score board for this sport:

Sport Study
Surfing

It's research time!
Use the Internet, books, tutorials and documentaries to study this sport. Or go see a game or competition!

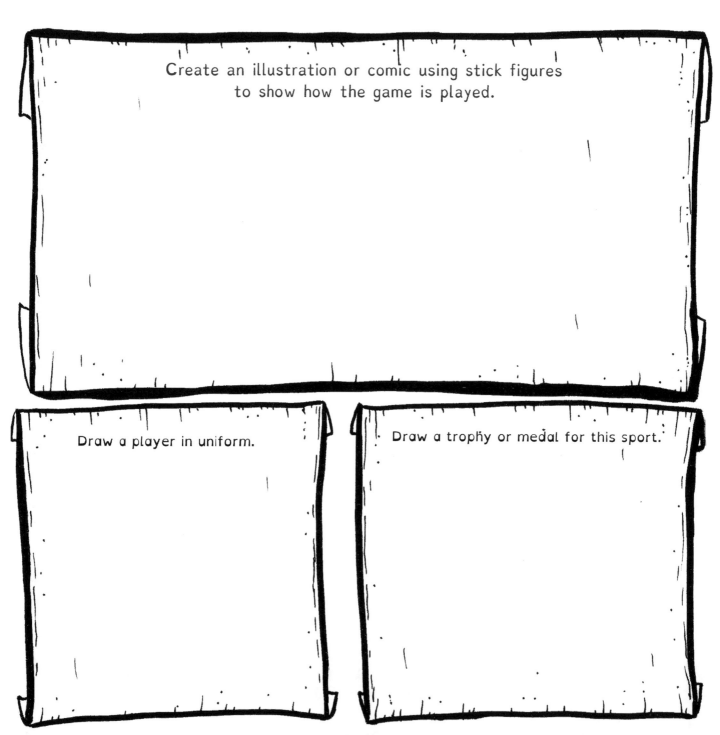

Create an illustration or comic using stick figures to show how the game is played.

Draw a player in uniform.

Draw a trophy or medal for this sport.

If you don't enjoy drawing, you may print, cut, and paste photos from the internet or a magazine onto this page.

Where did this sport originate?
_____
_____

How was this sport invented?
_____
_____
_____

Who are the main sponsors of the events for this sport?
_____
_____

What is the name of the largest competition where this sport is played? _____
_____
_____
_____
_____

Who is the #1 player of this sport? What makes them the best? How much money do they earn? Where do their earnings come from?
_____
_____
_____
_____

Would you like to play this sport? Why or why not?
_____
_____

What are the common injuries from playing this sport?
_____
_____
_____

What is a random fact about this sport?
_____
_____
_____

Table Tennis

Who were the winners in the most recent Olympics?

Medal	Men's Competition	Score	Women's Competition	Score
Gold				
Silver				
Bronze				

Research Challenge

Table Tennis
What is the 3 more common grips used in Table Tennis?

Design Challenge

Design a competition area, playing field, equipment, or score board for this sport:

Sport Study
Table Tennis

It's research time!
Use the Internet, books, tutorials and documentaries to study this sport. Or go see a game or competition!

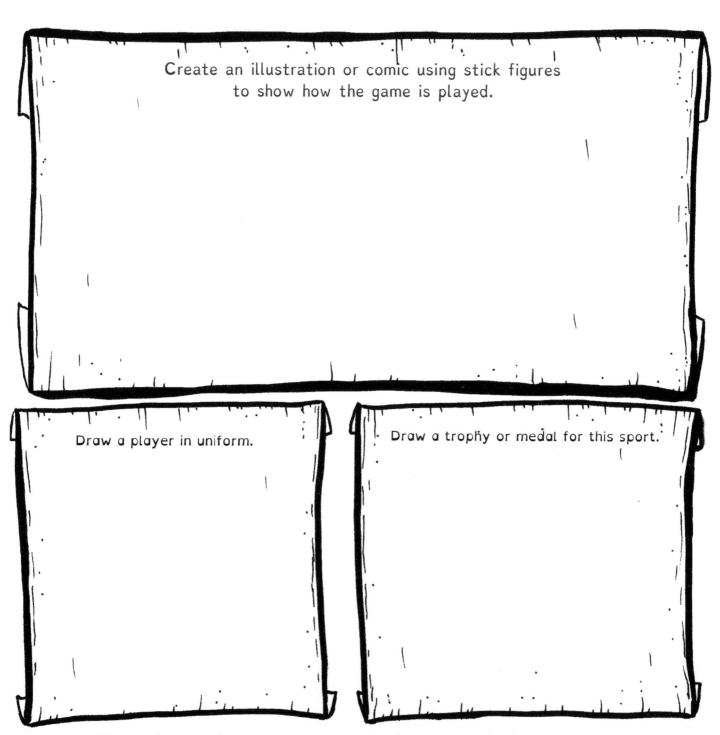

Create an illustration or comic using stick figures to show how the game is played.

Draw a player in uniform.

Draw a trophy or medal for this sport.

If you don't enjoy drawing, you may print, cut, and paste photos from the internet or a magazine onto this page.

Where did this sport originate?
_____
_____

How was this sport invented?
_____
_____
_____

Who are the main sponsors of the events for this sport?
_____
_____

What is the name of the largest competition where this sport is played? _____
_____
_____
_____
_____

Who is the #1 player of this sport? What makes them the best? How much money do they earn? Where do their earnings come from?
_____
_____
_____
_____

Would you like to play this sport? Why or why not?
_____
_____

What are the common injuries from playing this sport?
_____
_____
_____

What is a random fact about this sport?
_____
_____
_____

Tae Kwon Do

Who were the winners in the most recent Olympics?

Medal	Men's Competition	Score	Women's Competition	Score
Gold				
Silver				
Bronze				

Research Challenge

Tae Kwon Do
What does "Tae Kwon Do" translate to?

Design Challenge

Design a competition area, playing field, equipment, or score board for this sport:

Sport Study
Tae Kwon Do

It's research time!
Use the Internet, books, tutorials and documentaries to study this sport. Or go see a game or competition!

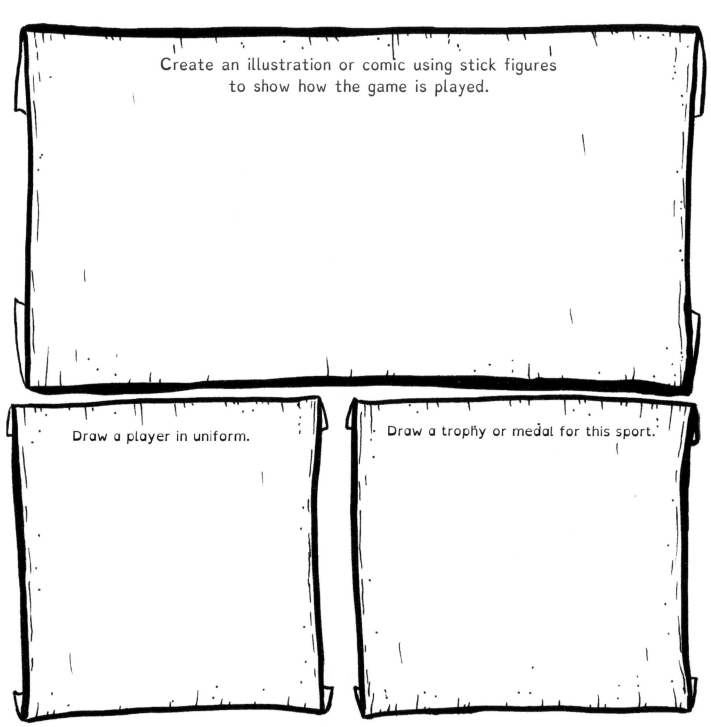

Create an illustration or comic using stick figures to show how the game is played.

Draw a player in uniform.

Draw a trophy or medal for this sport.

If you don't enjoy drawing, you may print, cut, and paste photos from the internet or a magazine onto this page.

Where did this sport originate?
_____
_____

How was this sport invented?
_____
_____
_____

Who are the main sponsors of the events for this sport?
_____
_____

What is the name of the largest competition where this sport is played? _____
_____
_____
_____
_____

Who is the #1 player of this sport? What makes them the best? How much money do they earn? Where do their earnings come from?
_____
_____
_____
_____

Would you like to play this sport? Why or why not?
_____
_____

What are the common injuries from playing this sport?
_____
_____
_____

What is a random fact about this sport?
_____
_____
_____

Tennis

Who were the winners in the most recent Olympics?

Medal	Men's Competition	Score	Women's Competition	Score
Gold				
Silver				
Bronze				

Research Challenge

Tennis
How does a player win a "Golden Slam"?

Design Challenge

Design a competition area, playing field, equipment, or score board for this sport:

Sport Study
Tennis

It's research time!
Use the Internet, books, tutorials and documentaries to study this sport. Or go see a game or competition!

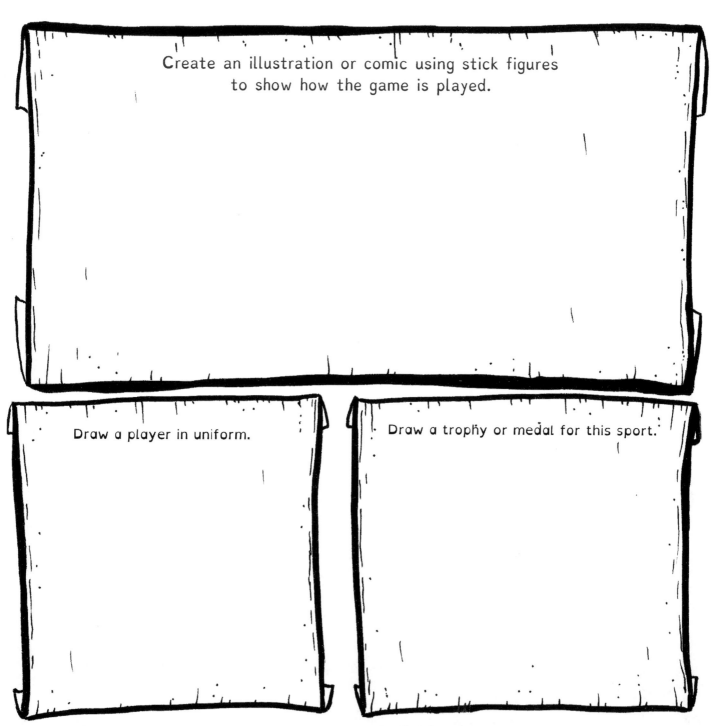

Create an illustration or comic using stick figures to show how the game is played.

Draw a player in uniform.

Draw a trophy or medal for this sport.

If you don't enjoy drawing, you may print, cut, and paste photos from the internet or a magazine onto this page.

Where did this sport originate?
_____
_____

How was this sport invented?
_____
_____
_____

Who are the main sponsors of the events for this sport?
_____
_____

What is the name of the largest competition where this sport is played? _____
_____
_____
_____
_____

Who is the #1 player of this sport? What makes them the best? How much money do they earn? Where do their earnings come from?
_____
_____
_____
_____

Would you like to play this sport? Why or why not?
_____
_____

What are the common injuries from playing this sport?
_____
_____
_____

What is a random fact about this sport?
_____
_____
_____

Track

Who were the winners in the most recent Olympics?

Medal	Men's Competition	Score	Women's Competition	Score
Gold				
Silver				
Bronze				

Research Challenge

Track
What three skills is Track based on?

_____
_____
_____
_____
_____

Design Challenge

Design a competition area, playing field, equipment, or score board for this sport:

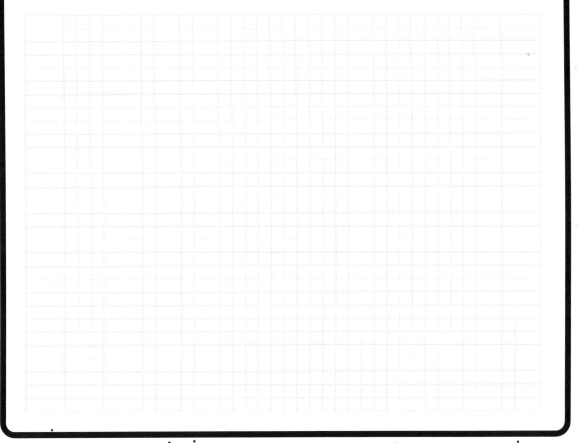

Sport Study
Track

It's research time!
Use the Internet, books, tutorials and documentaries to study this sport. Or go see a game or competition!

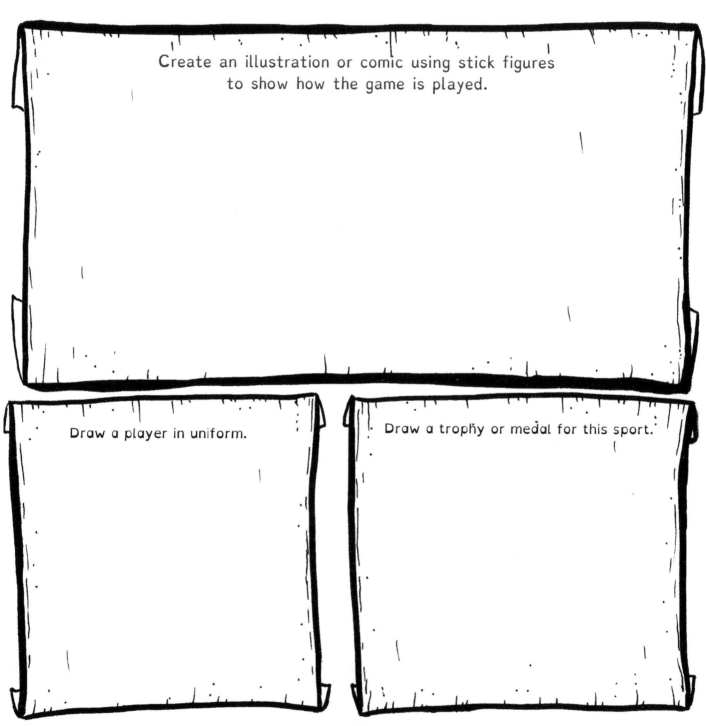

Create an illustration or comic using stick figures to show how the game is played.

Draw a player in uniform.

Draw a trophy or medal for this sport.

If you don't enjoy drawing, you may print, cut, and paste photos from the internet or a magazine onto this page.

Where did this sport originate?
_____
_____

How was this sport invented?
_____
_____
_____

Who are the main sponsors of the events for this sport?
_____
_____
_____

What is the name of the largest competition where this sport is played? _____
_____
_____
_____
_____
_____

Who is the #1 player of this sport? What makes them the best? How much money do they earn? Where do their earnings come from?
_____
_____
_____
_____

Would you like to play this sport? Why or why not?
_____
_____

What are the common injuries from playing this sport?
_____
_____
_____

What is a random fact about this sport?
_____
_____
_____

Track Cycling

Who were the winners in the most recent Olympics?

Medal	Men's Competition	Score	Women's Competition	Score
Gold				
Silver				
Bronze				

Research Challenge

Track Cycling
What are the 6 events of Track Cycling?

Design Challenge

Design a competition area, playing field, equipment, or score board for this sport:

Sport Study
Track Cycling

It's research time!
Use the Internet, books, tutorials and documentaries to study this sport. Or go see a game or competition!

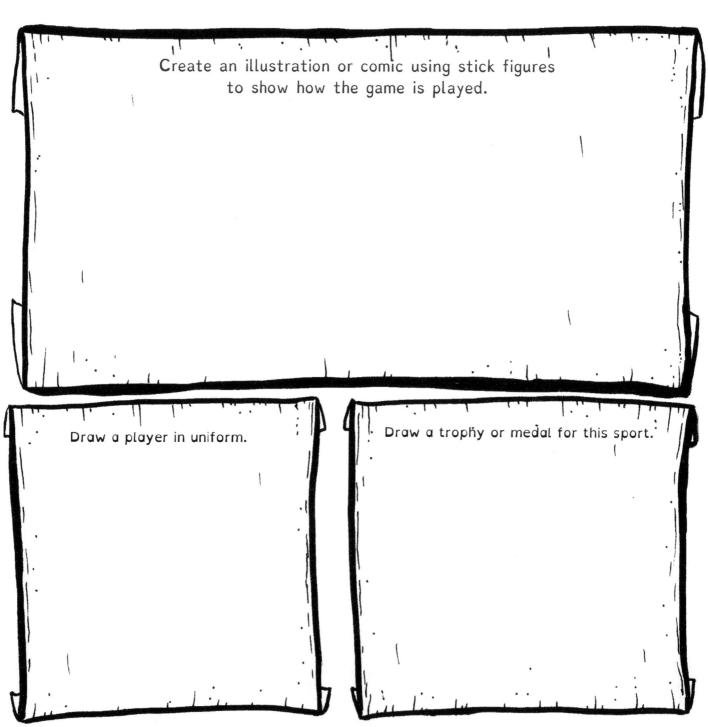

Create an illustration or comic using stick figures to show how the game is played.

Draw a player in uniform.

Draw a trophy or medal for this sport.

If you don't enjoy drawing, you may print, cut, and paste photos from the internet or a magazine onto this page.

Where did this sport originate?
_____
_____

How was this sport invented?
_____
_____
_____

Who are the main sponsors of the events for this sport?
_____
_____

What is the name of the largest competition where this sport is played? _____
_____
_____
_____
_____

Who is the #1 player of this sport? What makes them the best? How much money do they earn? Where do their earnings come from?
_____
_____
_____

Would you like to play this sport? Why or why not?
_____
_____

What are the common injuries from playing this sport?
_____
_____
_____

What is a random fact about this sport?
_____
_____
_____

Trampoline

Who were the winners in the most recent Olympics?

Medal	Men's Competition	Score	Women's Competition	Score
Gold				
Silver				
Bronze				

Research Challenge

Trampoline
Where must a Trampoline routine always start and finish?

_____
_____
_____
_____
_____
_____

Design Challenge

Design a competition area, playing field, equipment, or score board for this sport:

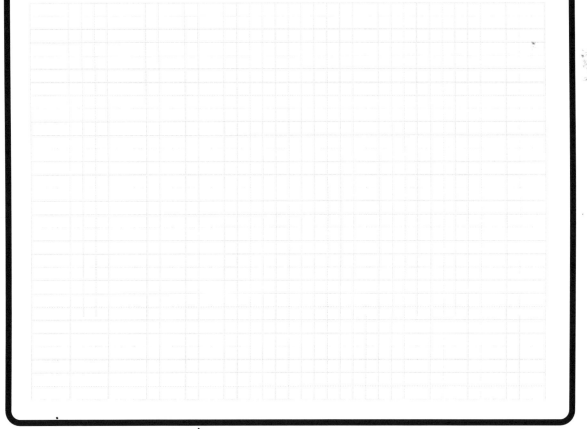

Sport Study
Trampoline

It's research time!
Use the Internet, books, tutorials and documentaries to study this sport. Or go see a game or competition!

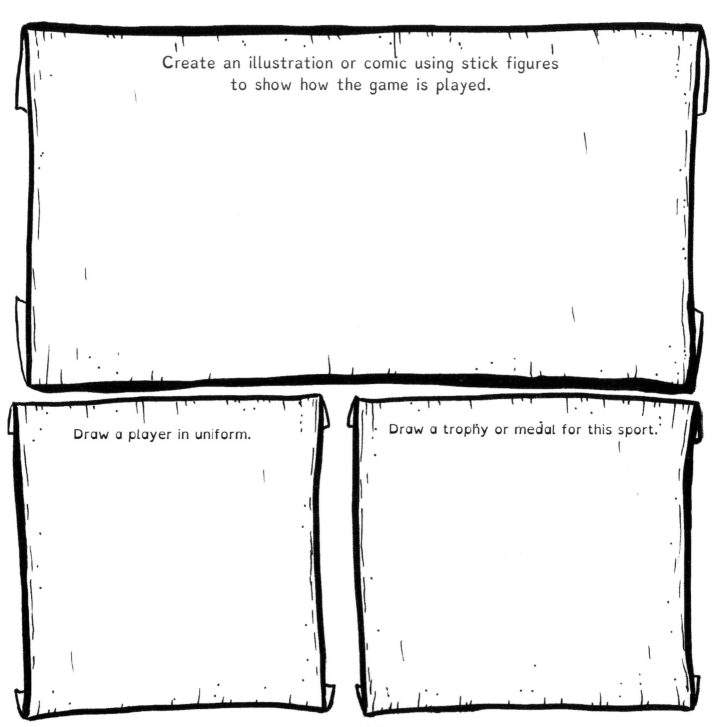

Create an illustration or comic using stick figures to show how the game is played.

Draw a player in uniform.

Draw a trophy or medal for this sport.

If you don't enjoy drawing, you may print, cut, and paste photos from the internet or a magazine onto this page.

Where did this sport originate?
_____
_____

How was this sport invented?
_____
_____
_____

Who are the main sponsors of the events for this sport?
_____
_____

What is the name of the largest competition where this sport is played? _____
_____
_____
_____
_____
_____

Who is the #1 player of this sport? What makes them the best? How much money do they earn? Where do their earnings come from?
_____
_____
_____
_____

Would you like to play this sport? Why or why not?
_____
_____

What are the common injuries from playing this sport?
_____
_____
_____

What is a random fact about this sport?
_____
_____
_____

Triathlon

Who were the winners in the most recent Olympics?

Medal	Men's Competition	Score	Women's Competition	Score
Gold				
Silver				
Bronze				

Research Challenge

Triathlon
What three events make up a Triathlon?

_____
_____
_____
_____
_____
_____

Design Challenge

Design a competition area, playing field, equipment, or score board for this sport:

Sport Study
Triathlon

It's research time!
Use the Internet, books, tutorials and documentaries to study this sport. Or go see a game or competition!

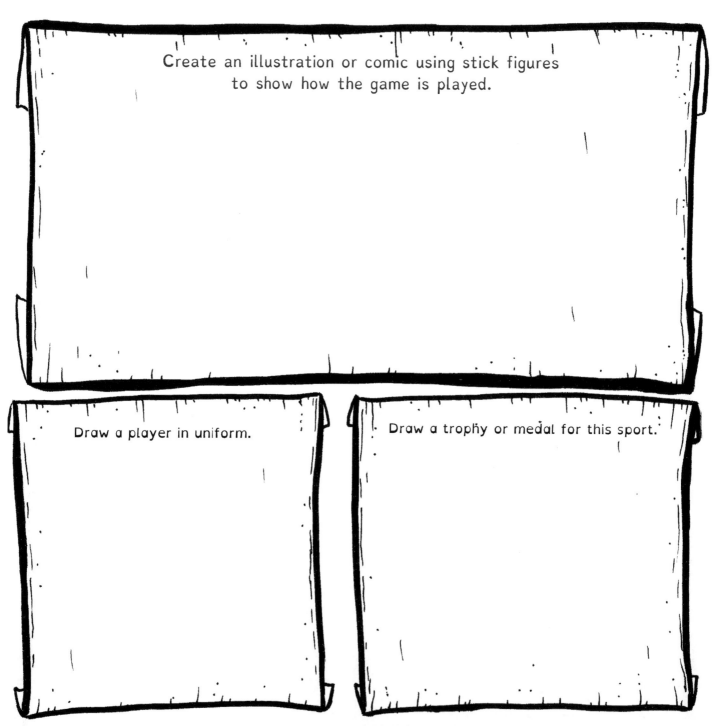

Create an illustration or comic using stick figures to show how the game is played.

Draw a player in uniform.

Draw a trophy or medal for this sport.

If you don't enjoy drawing, you may print, cut, and paste photos from the internet or a magazine onto this page.

Where did this sport originate?
_____
_____

How was this sport invented?
_____
_____
_____

Who are the main sponsors of the events for this sport?
_____
_____

What is the name of the largest competition where this sport is played? _____
_____
_____
_____
_____

Who is the #1 player of this sport? What makes them the best? How much money do they earn? Where do their earnings come from?
_____
_____
_____
_____

Would you like to play this sport? Why or why not?
_____
_____

What are the common injuries from playing this sport?
_____
_____
_____

What is a random fact about this sport?
_____
_____
_____

Volleyball

Who were the winners in the most recent Olympics?

Medal	Men's Competition	Score	Women's Competition	Score
Gold				
Silver				
Bronze				

Research Challenge

Volleyball
How many players are on each side of the court and what is the maximum number of hits per side?

___

Design Challenge

Design a competition area, playing field, equipment, or score board for this sport:

Sport Study
Volleyball

It's research time!
Use the Internet, books, tutorials and documentaries to study this sport. Or go see a game or competition!

Create an illustration or comic using stick figures to show how the game is played.

Draw a player in uniform.

Draw a trophy or medal for this sport.

If you don't enjoy drawing, you may print, cut, and paste photos from the internet or a magazine onto this page.

Where did this sport originate?
_____
_____

How was this sport invented?
_____
_____
_____

Who are the main sponsors of the events for this sport?
_____
_____

What is the name of the largest competition where this sport is played? _____
_____
_____
_____
_____
_____

Who is the #1 player of this sport? What makes them the best? How much money do they earn? Where do their earnings come from?
_____
_____
_____
_____

Would you like to play this sport? Why or why not?
_____
_____

What are the common injuries from playing this sport?
_____
_____

What is a random fact about this sport?
_____
_____

Water Polo

Who were the winners in the most recent Olympics?

Medal	Men's Competition	Score	Women's Competition	Score
Gold				
Silver				
Bronze				

Research Challenge

Water Polo
How deep is the water in the pool for Water Polo?
Can players feet touch the bottom?

_____
_____
_____
_____
_____
_____
_____

Design Challenge

Design a competition area, playing field, equipment,
or score board for this sport:

Sport Study
Water Polo

It's research time!
Use the Internet, books, tutorials and documentaries to study this sport. Or go see a game or competition!

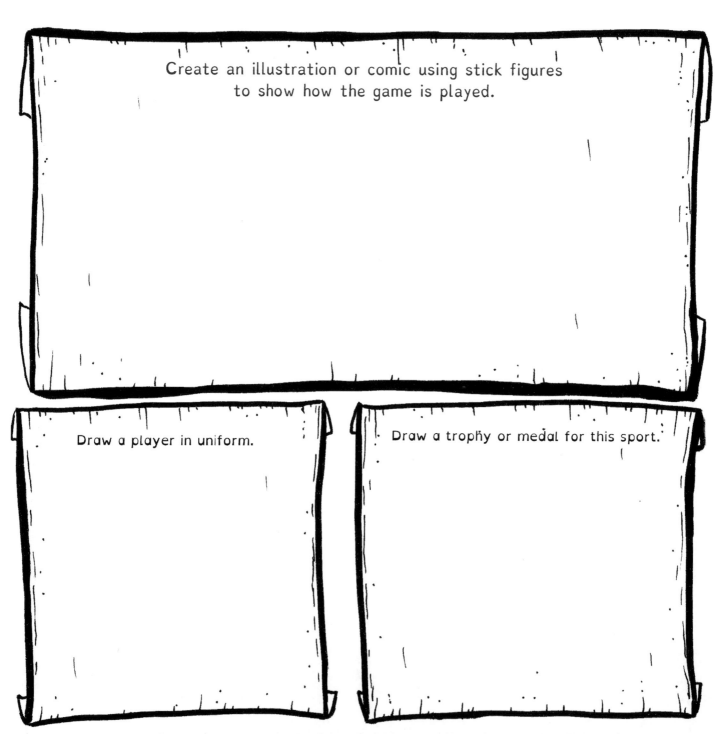

Create an illustration or comic using stick figures to show how the game is played.

Draw a player in uniform.

Draw a trophy or medal for this sport.

If you don't enjoy drawing, you may print, cut, and paste photos from the internet or a magazine onto this page.

Where did this sport originate?
_____
_____

How was this sport invented?
_____
_____
_____

Who are the main sponsors of the events for this sport?
_____
_____

What is the name of the largest competition where this sport is played? _____
_____
_____
_____
_____

Who is the #1 player of this sport? What makes them the best? How much money do they earn? Where do their earnings come from?
_____
_____
_____
_____

Would you like to play this sport? Why or why not?
_____
_____

What are the common injuries from playing this sport?
_____
_____
_____

What is a random fact about this sport?
_____
_____
_____

Weightlifting

Who were the winners in the most recent Olympics?

Medal	Men's Competition	Score	Women's Competition	Score
Gold				
Silver				
Bronze				

Research Challenge

Weightlifting
In what year were weight classes separated and how many weight classes does the Weightlifting competition cover?

Design Challenge

Design a competition area, playing field, equipment, or score board for this sport:

Sport Study
Weightlifting

It's research time!
Use the Internet, books, tutorials and documentaries to study this sport. Or go see a game or competition!

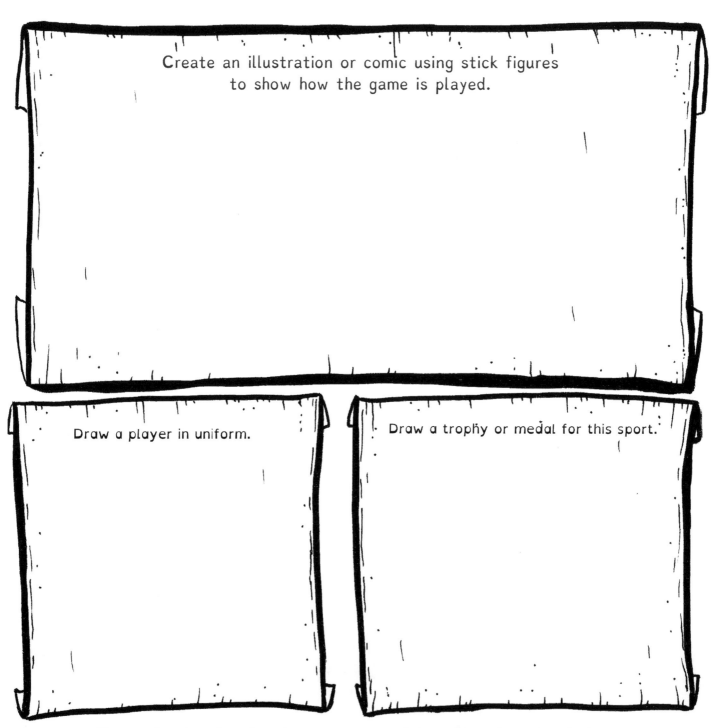

Create an illustration or comic using stick figures to show how the game is played.

Draw a player in uniform.

Draw a trophy or medal for this sport.

If you don't enjoy drawing, you may print, cut, and paste photos from the internet or a magazine onto this page.

Where did this sport originate?
_____
_____

How was this sport invented?
_____
_____
_____

Who are the main sponsors of the events for this sport?
_____
_____
_____

What is the name of the largest competition where this sport is played? _____
_____
_____
_____
_____
_____
_____

Who is the #1 player of this sport? What makes them the best? How much money do they earn? Where do their earnings come from?
_____
_____
_____
_____

Would you like to play this sport? Why or why not?
_____
_____

What are the common injuries from playing this sport?
_____
_____
_____

What is a random fact about this sport?
_____
_____
_____

Wrestling

Who were the winners in the most recent Olympics?

Medal	Men's Competition	Score	Women's Competition	Score
Gold				
Silver				
Bronze				

Research Challenge

Wrestling

What two types of Wrestling are represented in the Olympics? Explain some differences between the two.

Design Challenge

Design a competition area, playing field, equipment, or score board for this sport:

Sport Study
Wrestling

It's research time!
Use the Internet, books, tutorials and documentaries to study this sport. Or go see a game or competition!

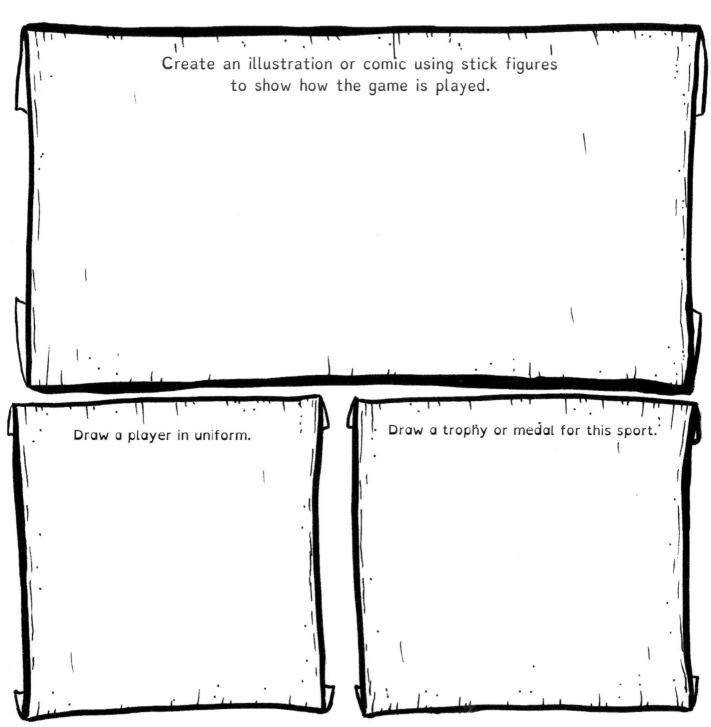

Create an illustration or comic using stick figures to show how the game is played.

Draw a player in uniform.

Draw a trophy or medal for this sport.

If you don't enjoy drawing, you may print, cut, and paste photos from the internet or a magazine onto this page.

Where did this sport originate?
_____
_____

How was this sport invented?
_____
_____
_____

Who are the main sponsors of the events for this sport?
_____
_____

What is the name of the largest competition where this sport is played? _____
_____
_____
_____
_____

Who is the #1 player of this sport? What makes them the best? How much money do they earn? Where do their earnings come from?
_____
_____
_____
_____

Would you like to play this sport? Why or why not?
_____
_____

What are the common injuries from playing this sport?
_____
_____
_____

What is a random fact about this sport?
_____
_____
_____

Choose your own sport!

Who were the winners in the most recent Olympics?

Medal	Men's Competition	Score	Women's Competition	Score
Gold				
Silver				
Bronze				

Research Challenge

What are the rules of the game?

Design Challenge

Design a competition area, playing field, equipment, or score board for this sport:

Sport Study

It's research time!
Use the Internet, books, tutorials and documentaries to study this sport. Or go see a game or competition!

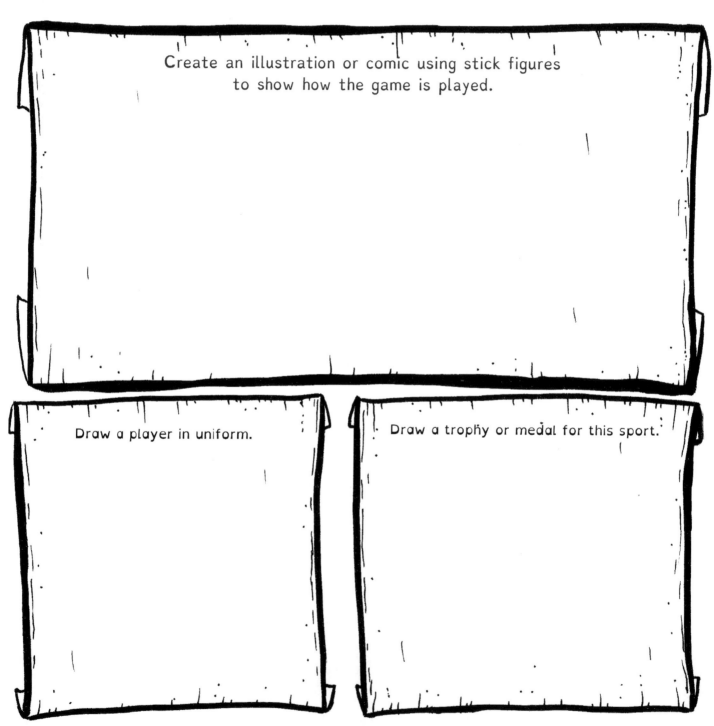

Create an illustration or comic using stick figures to show how the game is played.

Draw a player in uniform.

Draw a trophy or medal for this sport.

If you don't enjoy drawing, you may print, cut, and paste photos from the internet or a magazine onto this page.

Where did this sport originate?
_____
_____

How was this sport invented?
_____
_____
_____

Who are the main sponsors of the events for this sport?
_____
_____

What is the name of the largest competition where this sport is played? _____
_____
_____
_____
_____

Who is the #1 player of this sport? What makes them the best? How much money do they earn? Where do their earnings come from?
_____
_____
_____
_____

Would you like to play this sport? Why or why not?
_____
_____

What are the common injuries from playing this sport?
_____
_____
_____

What is a random fact about this sport?
_____
_____
_____

Who were the winners in the most recent Olympics?

Medal	Men's Competition	Score	Women's Competition	Score
Gold				
Silver				
Bronze				

Research Challenge

What are the rules of the game?

_____
_____
_____
_____
_____
_____
_____

Design Challenge

Design a competition area, playing field, equipment, or score board for this sport:

Sport Study

It's research time!
Use the Internet, books, tutorials and documentaries to study this sport. Or go see a game or competition!

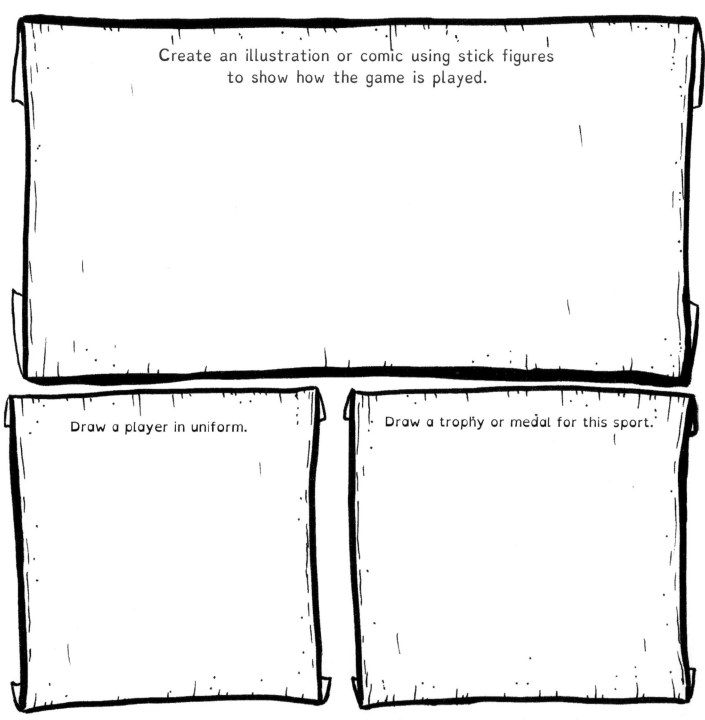

Create an illustration or comic using stick figures to show how the game is played.

Draw a player in uniform.

Draw a trophy or medal for this sport.

If you don't enjoy drawing, you may print, cut, and paste photos from the internet or a magazine onto this page.

Where did this sport originate?
_____
_____

How was this sport invented?
_____
_____
_____

Who are the main sponsors of the events for this sport?
_____
_____

What is the name of the largest competition where this sport is played? _____
_____
_____
_____
_____
_____

Who is the #1 player of this sport? What makes them the best? How much money do they earn? Where do their earnings come from?
_____
_____
_____
_____

Would you like to play this sport? Why or why not?
_____
_____

What are the common injuries from playing this sport?
_____
_____
_____

What is a random fact about this sport?
_____
_____
_____

Who were the winners in the most recent Olympics?

Medal	Men's Competition	Score	Women's Competition	Score
Gold				
Silver				
Bronze				

Research Challenge

What are the rules of the game?

Design Challenge

Design a competition area, playing field, equipment, or score board for this sport:

Sport Study

It's research time!
Use the Internet, books, tutorials and documentaries to study this sport. Or go see a game or competition!

Create an illustration or comic using stick figures to show how the game is played.

Draw a player in uniform.

Draw a trophy or medal for this sport.

If you don't enjoy drawing, you may print, cut, and paste photos from the internet or a magazine onto this page.

Where did this sport originate?
_____
_____

How was this sport invented?
_____
_____
_____

Who are the main sponsors of the events for this sport?
_____
_____

What is the name of the largest competition where this sport is played? _____
_____
_____
_____
_____
_____

Who is the #1 player of this sport? What makes them the best? How much money do they earn? Where do their earnings come from?
_____
_____
_____
_____

Would you like to play this sport? Why or why not?
_____
_____

What are the common injuries from playing this sport?
_____
_____
_____

What is a random fact about this sport?
_____
_____
_____

The Thinking Tree
OLYMPICS SPORTS
Math Mysteries

You may wish to use a calculator to find the answers.

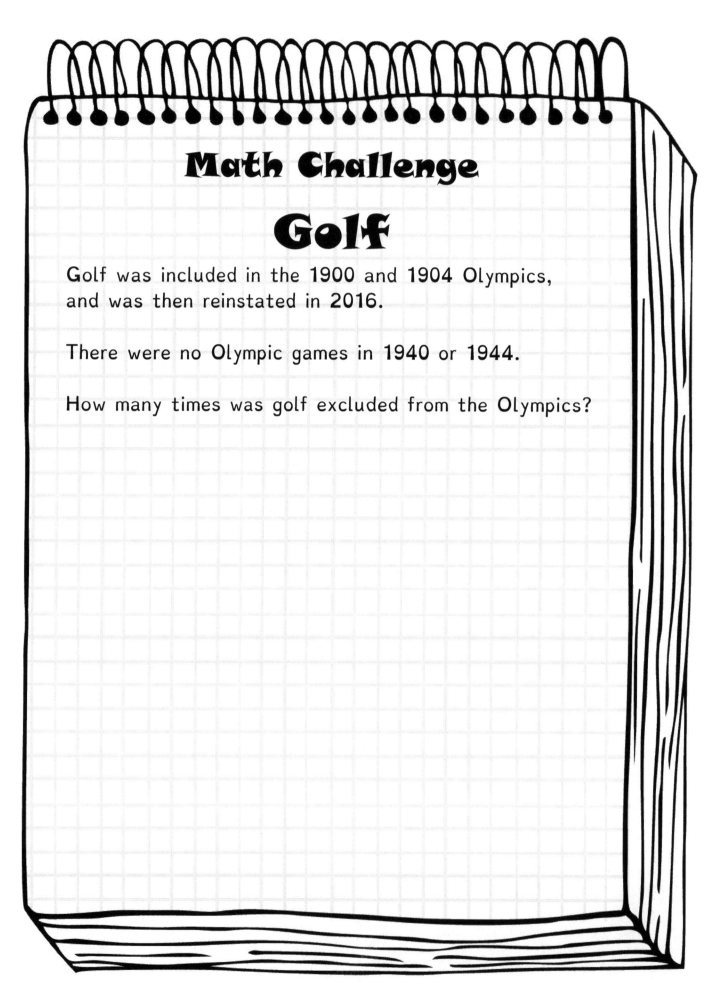

Math Challenge

Golf

Golf was included in the 1900 and 1904 Olympics, and was then reinstated in 2016.

There were no Olympic games in 1940 or 1944.

How many times was golf excluded from the Olympics?

Math Challenge

Nordic Combined

During the team event, there are four team members, and they cover a total of **20** km during the cross country portion of the race.

How many km does each member ski during the relay?

Math Challenge

Archery

The archer shoots 72 arrows during the qualification phase of the Olympics.

If the best score the archer can get per arrow is 10, what is the highest score the archer can earn?

Math Challenge
Bobsleigh

Add the run times and determine the winner.

Bobsleigh A: 46.71 seconds 46.64 seconds 46.84 seconds 47.32 seconds

Bobsleigh B: 46.71 seconds 46.93 seconds 47.33 seconds 47.62 seconds

Who is the winner?

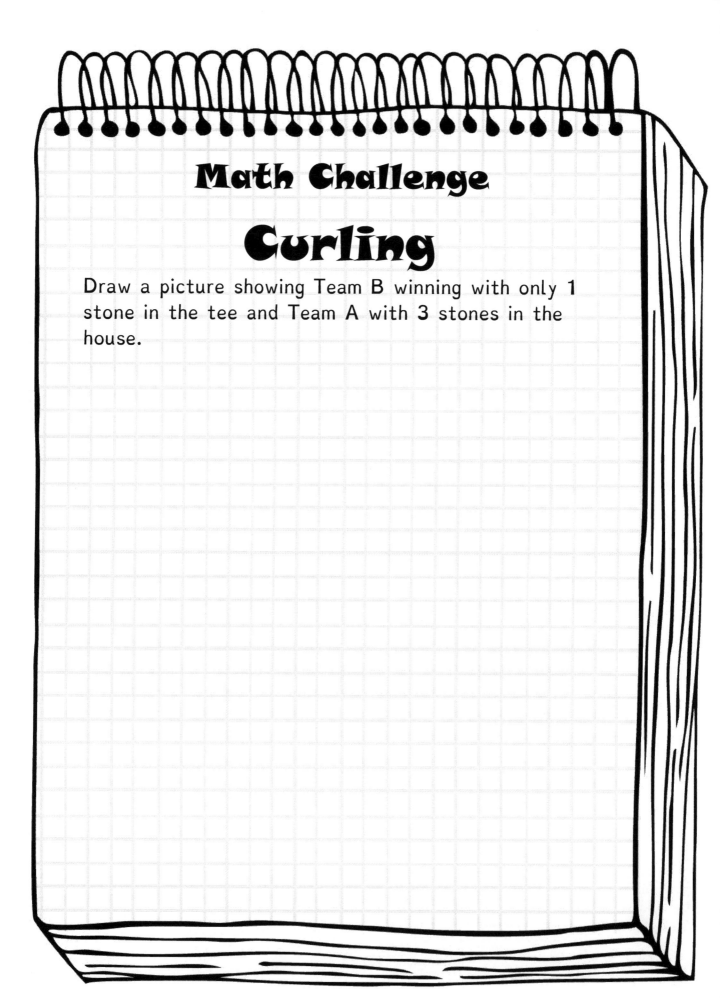

Math Challenge

Curling

Draw a picture showing Team B winning with only **1** stone in the tee and Team A with **3** stones in the house.

Math Challenge

Weightlifting

The standard weightlifting bar is **45** lbs (**20** kg).

If the lifter is lifting **265** lbs (**120** kg), how much weight is added to each side of the bar?

Math Challenge

Track

Four women are running the **4X100** meter relay. How long does it take to complete the race if these are their times?

12.5 seconds

11.2 seconds

11.9 seconds

10.9 seconds

Math Challenge

Swimming

A marathon swimming race is 10 km long.
One of the shortest races is 100 m.

What is the difference in distance between these two races?

The freestyle relay is done at two different distances. There is the 4 X 100 m and 4 X 200 m.

What is the total distance covered in the 4 X 100 m?

What is the total distance covered in the 4 X 200 m?

What is the difference between these totals?

Math Challenge
Luge

The track for luge men's singles is **1,365** meters. The luge track for men's doubles is **1,065** meters.

How much longer is the singles track?

Math Challenge

Snowboarding

Snowboarding was first introduced to the Olympics in 1998. The Olympics happen every four years.

How many times (including this year) has snowboarding been an Olympic sport?

Math Challenge
Boxing

There are 12 rounds.
If a boxer wins a round, he gets 10 points.
If he loses a round, he gets 9 points.
If a boxer gets knocked down once in the round, he would get 8 points.
If he gets knocked down twice in the round, he would get 7 points.

Boxer A won 7 rounds and was knocked down twice in one round he lost. How many points did he score?

Boxer B won 5 rounds and was not knocked down in the rounds he lost. How many points did he score?

Who is the winner?

Math Challenge
Hockey

Hockey has three 20 minute periods and a 15 minute intermission between periods.

How long are the players on the ice during a game?

How long is the game including the intermissions?

If you are familiar with hockey, does the game usually last this long, or are they usually longer?

Math Challenge
Rugby

There are five different ways to score in Rugby.
Find the points awarded for each.

Try_____
Conversion_____
Penalty Goal_____
Drop Goal_____
Penalty Try_____

If Team A scores 3 tries, 2 conversions, and 1 penalty try, what is their score?

If Team B scores 4 tries, 1 conversion, and 1 penalty goal, what is their score?

Which team wins?

Math Challenge
Swimming

A Marathon Swimming race is 10 km long. One of the shortest races is 100 m.

What is the difference in distance between these two races?

The freestyle relay is done at two different distances.

There is the 4 X 100 m and 4 X 200 m.

What is the total distance covered in the 4 X 100 m?

What is the total distance covered in the 4 X 200 m?

What is the difference between these totals?

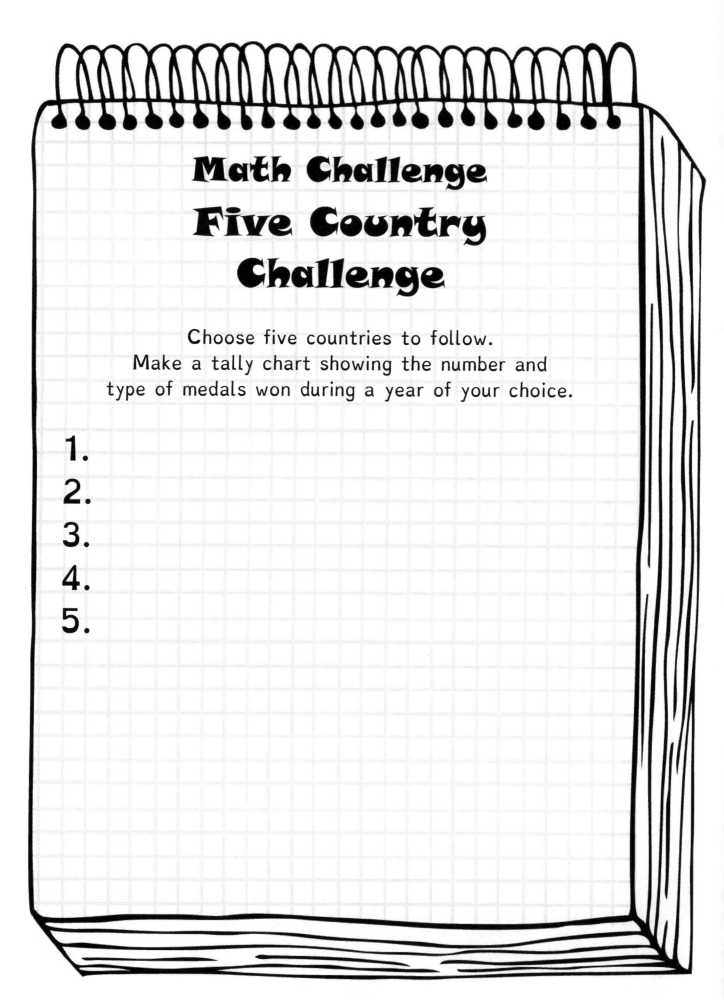

Math Challenge
Five Country Challenge

Choose five countries to follow.
Make a tally chart showing the number and
type of medals won during a year of your choice.

1.
2.
3.
4.
5.

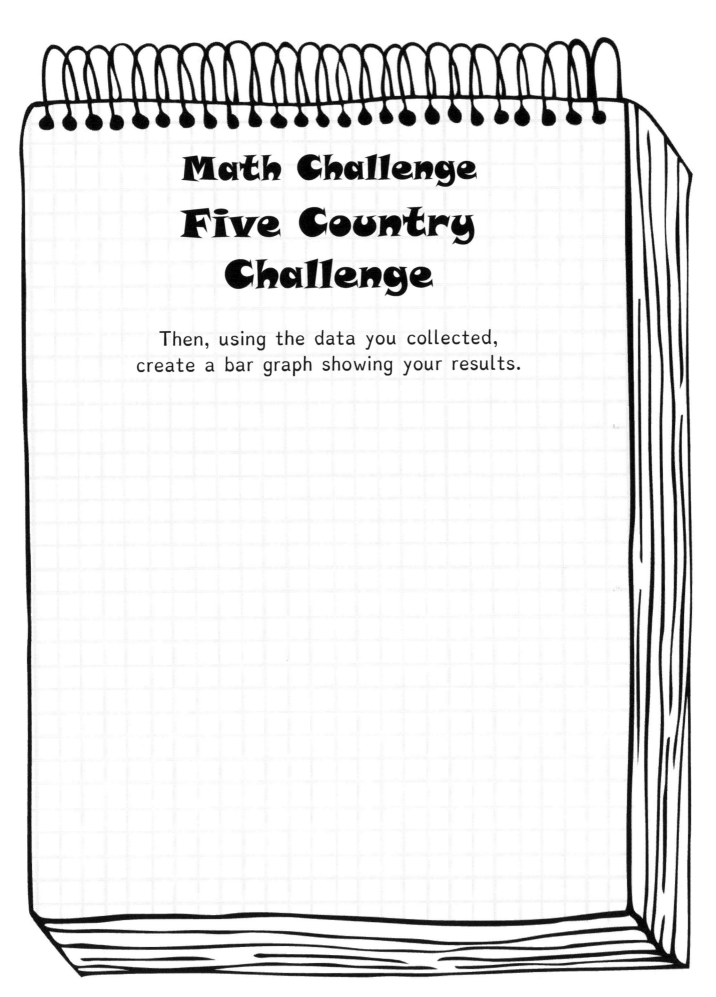

Math Challenge
Five Country Challenge

Then, using the data you collected, create a bar graph showing your results.

What Five Olympic Sports Do You Like Best? Explain Why.

1. _____

2. _____

3. _____

4. _____

5. _____

Notes & Doodles

The Thinking Tree
RESEARCH CHALLENGE
ANSWER KEY

No Cheating.

Please do your own research.

Research Challenge—Questions & Answers

Acrobatic Gymnastics
Q. What is the code of points and how has it changed over the years?
A. A rule book that defines the scoring system for each level of competition.

Alpine Skiing
Q. What is the primary difference between Alpine Skiing and other types of skiing?
A. Alpine skiing consists of wearing fixed-heel bindings rather than free-heel bindings.

Archery
Q. How many circles are on an Olympic target and how large in diameter is the target face?
A. 10, 48 inches

Artistic Gymnastics
Q. What three things are both male and female gymnasts judged on?
A. Execution, Degree of difficulty, and overall presentation.

Artistic Swimming
Q. What is another name for Artistic Swimming? What other name was it known by?
A. Synchronized Swimming, Water Ballet

Athletics
Q. What three types of events are included in Athletics?
A. Track and field events, road running, and race walking.

Badminton
Q. What kind of scoring is used for Badminton? What does this mean?
A. Rally Scoring, It means the player does not need to be serving to score. Player must win by two points or be the first to score 30 points.

Baseball
Q. How are the qualifying teams decided for the Olympic games? Do you think this is fair?
A. Hosting nation always gets a spot, the other 7 are chosen by continental qualifying tournaments

Basketball
Q. What is a technical foul? How do you get one? What happens when the referee calls one against your team?
A. Answers may vary.

Beach Handball
Q. How does beach handball differ from standard handball? Do you think this makes it easier or more difficult?
A. It is played on sand instead of a solid floor, there is also more passing instead of dribbling.

Beach Volleyball
Q. How many teams take part in the Beach Volleyball tournament and is there a limit of teams for each country?
A. 24, two per country

Biathalon
Q. What two sports are combined to create the Biathlon competition?
A. Cross country skiing and rifle shooting.

BMX Freestyle
Q. Can you list 5 air tricks and 5 flatland tricks that an Olympian might use in the BMX Freestyle competition?
A. Answers will vary.

BMX Racing-
Q. What are the three different rounds in the BMX Racing competition and how many cyclists compete in each?
A. Quarterfinals-24, Semi Finals-16, and Final -8.

Bobsleigh
Q. Since being introduced at the 1912 games what is the only year that this event has not been featured and why?
A. In 1960, Squaw Valley the committee opted to not build a track to reduce their expenses.

Boxing
Q. What year did the Olympics incorporate women's boxing as an Olympic event in addition to men's and how many weight classes does each consist of?
A. 2012, 8 for men 5 for women

Breaking
Q. What was the first year that Olympics introduced breaking (or breakdancing) to the summer Olympic program and how many were competing?
A. 2024, 16 boys and 16 girls

Canoe/Kayak Flatwater
Q. What are the distances for each of the Canoe/Kayak Flatwater courses?
A. 200-meter, 500-meter, 1000-meter

Canoe/Kayak Slalom
Q. What is the difference between canoe and kayak slalom?
A. Slalom kayaks are paddled sitting down, with legs stretched in front. Slalom canoes are paddled while kneeling in the kayak.

Curling
Q. What are the different parts of a curling sheet?
A. Centreline, Hogline, Teeline, Backline, Hack Line with Hacks, and Free Guard Zone

Diving
Q. How many different events are included at the Olympic Diving competitions? What are they?
A. 8 total, 4 women's, and 4 men's. 3m springboard, synchronized 3m springboard, 10m platform, and synchronized 10m platform

Fencing
Q. What are 3 types of Olympic Fencing? Give a brief description of each.
A. Foile-light thrusting weapon, target is torso
Epee-heavy thrusting weapon, target is entire body
Sabre- light cutting and thrusting weapon, target is almost everything above the waist

Figure Skating
Q. What are the different medaled events for Figure Skating?
A. Men's singles, men's special figures, ladie's singles, pair skating, ice dance, and mixed team.

Football (Soccer)
Q. What is the maximum age of male competitors and are there any exceptions?
A. 23, a maximum of 3 over 23 may participate.

Freestyle Skiing
Q. What are the six different events that make up Olympic Freestyle Skiing? Which do you think takes the most skill?
A. Aerials, Moguls, Cross, Half-Pipe, slopestyle, and Big Air.

Futsal
Q. How is Futsal different from Football?
A. It is played on a hard court mainly indoors instead of on a football pitch and the playing area is smaller.

Golf
Q. How does a competitor qualify to compete in Olympic golf?
A. The top 15 of each gender from the Official World Golf Ranking and Women's World Golf Rankings are automatically qualified for competition with a limit of four per country.

Handball
Q. How long does a handball match last?
A. Two 30 minute halves with a 10 or 15 minute halftime intermission.

Hockey
Q. What are the two styles of hockey played in the Olympics and when are they played?
A. Field Hockey- Summer, Ice Hockey- Winter

Karate
Q. What are the two types of karate that are used in the Olympics and how many competitors are on the mat for each?
A. Kata- solo, Kumite-sparring with an opponent

Luge
Q. What are the 4 different Luge disciplines?
A. Men's singles, doubles open to both sexes, women's singles, and team relay.

Q. Marathon Swimming
What is the minimum distance for the Marathon Swimming event in the Olympics and approximately how long does it take ?
A. 10 kilometers (6.21 miles), 1 ½ to 2 hours.

Modern Pentathlon
Q. What are the 5 different events that make up the Modern Pentathlon?
A. Fencing, free style swimming, equestrian show jumping, and combined final event of pistol shooting and cross country running.

Mountain Bike
Q. What are some special features of mountain bikes that differ from other bikes to make them able to perform better on rough terrain?
A. Air or coil spring shocks for suspension, larger and wider wheels, stronger frames, and mechanically or hydraulically actuated disc brakes.

Nordic Combined
Q. Nordic Combined is a mixture of which two sports?
A. Cross-country skiing and ski jumping.

Roller Speed Skating
Q. What is the average speed in Roller Speed Skating?
A. 40+ mph

Rowing
Q. How many oars are used in each of the two types of Rowing- Sweep rowing and sculling?
A. 1, 2

Rugby
Q. How many players and how many substitutes play in an Olympic Rugby match?
A. 7 per side and 5 substitutes

Shooting
Q. How many Shooting events are included in the Olympic events?
A. 15, 6 men's, 6 women's, and 3 mixed events.

Short Track Speed Skating
Q. In Short Track Speed Skating what does the term "Impeding" mean?
A. Intentionally pushing, blocking, tripping, or causing impediment for another skater.

Skateboarding

Q. Are Olympic participants required to wear helmets during Skateboarding competitions? Do you agree with this, why or why not?
A. Only those under 18 are required to wear helmets, Answers will vary.

Skeleton

Q. What is the only nation that has won a metal every time that Skeleton was a feature in the Olympic competition?
A. Great Britain

Ski Jumping

Q. What three parts does the Ski Jumping venue consist of?
A. Jumping ramp, take-off table, and landing hill.

Ski Mountaineering

Q. What are some equipment items that you would need for this activity?
A. Bindings, boots, skis, ski skins, rope, crampons, ice axe.

Snowboarding

Q. Can you list all the different styles of Snowboarding?
A. Jibbing, Freeriding, freestyle, alpine snowboarding, slopestyle, big air, half pipe, snowboard cross, snowboard racing.

Speed Skating

Q. What year did Speed Skating make its Olympic debut?
A. 1924

Sport Climbing

Q. What does the Sport Climbing term "abseiling" mean?
A. A controlled descent off a vertical drop.

Surfing

Q. What are the three major subdivisions in Stand Up Surfing?
A. Stand-up paddling, long boarding, and shortboarding.

Table Tennis

Q. What is the 3 most common grips used in Table Tennis?
A. Shakehand Grip, Penhold, and Seemiller

Tae Kwon Do

Q. What does "Tae Kwon Do" translate to?
A. Kicking, punching, the art or way of.

Track Cycling
Q. What are the 6 events of Track Cycling?
A. Team sprint, match sprint, keirin, omnium, team pursuit, and madison.

Track
Q. What three skills is Track based on?
A. Running, jumping, and throwing.

Trampoline
Q. Where must a Trampoline routine always start and finish?
A. On your feet

Triathlon
Q. What three events make up a Triathlon?
A. Swimming, cycling, running.

Volleyball
Q. How many players are on each side of the court and what is the maximum number of hits per side?
A. 6,3

Water Polo
Q. How deep is the water in the pool for Water Polo? Can players feet touch the bottom?
A. 6.5 feet, no

Weightlifting
Q. In what year were weight classes separated and how many weight classes does the Weightlifting competition cover?
A. 1920, 5

Wrestling
Q. What two types of Wrestling are represented in the Olympics? Explain some differences between the two.
A. Greco Roman and freestyle. Answers will vary.

FunSchooling.com
Copyright 2022 - Copies allowed for Household Use
The Thinking Tree, LLC

Made in the USA
Columbia, SC
13 February 2023

12217128R00165